THE ANT IN THE EAR OF THE ELEPHANT

The story of the people's struggle
against the Koodankulam nuclear plant

Minnie Vaid

rajpal

₹ 325

ISBN : 9789350643969

Ist Edition : 2016 © Rajpal & Sons

THE ANT IN THE EAR OF THE ELEPHANT

by Minnie Vaid

Cover design : Sakshi Chopra Kumar

Cover photograph : Amirtharaj Stephen

Printed at G.H. Prints (P) Ltd., Delhi

RAJPAL & SONS

1590, Madarsa Road, Kashmere Gate, Delhi-110006

Phone : 011-23869812, 23865483, Fax : 011-23867791

e-mail : sales@rajpalpublishing.com

www.rajpalpublishing.com

www.facebook.com/rajpalandsons

For my parents
Dr Jawaharlal Vaid
and
Mrs Prem Vaid

Acknowledgements

This is probably the toughest piece of writing I have ever undertaken and I would like to thank my family in Pune for giving me the space and support-quite literally-to be able to reach the finish line.

I had visions of myself at age 80 still writing about the Koodankulam nuclear power plant; I certainly hope the people sitting on protest against it, do not have similar fears regarding the outcome of their struggle.

Translator Amal Raj Leon deserves a special thank you for his indefatigable help in Idinthakarai and later on also, patiently answering queries and sending documents. Thanks to Nishtha Balagopal for Tamil translations/transcriptions in Mumbai.

I would also like to thank Rohit Gosalia for clarifying sundry points of science that were-and remain-incomprehensible to a right-brained person like me.

Most of all, for listening patiently and uncomplainingly for the better part of two years, grateful thanks to Palpaysam, now and always.

•

Contents

Chapter One
Introduction   11

Chapter Two
A Nuclear Plant In Your Backyard   25

Chapter Three
Living in Exile: Leaders of A
Lonely Movement   49

Chapter Four
"A Jail Within, A Jail Without"
or The September 2012 Siege   80

Chapter Five
Chinks In The Koodankulam Armour   108

Chapter Six
Life After The Plant Goes 'Critical'   149

Chapter Seven
Journey's End Or New Beginnings?   185

Epilogue   216

Publisher's Note   223

References   227

Chapter One

INTRODUCTION

"If you are to suffer, you should suffer in the interest of the country."
—Jawaharlal Nehru, speaking to villagers who were to
be displaced by the Hirakud Dam, 1948 (as quoted in 'For
the Greater Common Good', by Arundhati Roy, *Outlook*
magazine, May 24,1999)

June 2013

It's almost a sci-fi moment: a quiet, undisturbed countryside,
a few cows placidly grazing near some hutments, children
playing in the distance against a backdrop of towering 80-metre
Suzlon windmills slicing the air. The car driver, who has shared
an amiable journey with me in silence for almost three hours,
now pipes in to say succinctly: "Current." That's the extent of his
English. My Tamil isn't much better. I nod companionably.

The drive from Thiruvananthapuram airport to
Koodankulam, 110-odd kilometres away, is predictably scenic.
An unending canopy of coconut trees gives the impression of
continuous green foliage with hilly rocks reaching for the skies.
A little later, the occasional windmills transform into a whole

army of them, some moving impressively fast, others not at all. Wind energy versus nuclear energy? I start thinking of the reason I am travelling to Idinthakarai, a small fishing village in coastal Tamil Nadu, the epicentre of an ongoing two-and-a-half-year people's movement against the Koodankulam nuclear reactor in Radhapuram taluka of Tamil Nadu's Tirunelveli district.

As the car brakes to a halt in front of the parish priest's residence, the first thing I notice is, the enormous *pandal* (tent) opposite, in front of the impressive grey arches of the Lourdes Matha church.

Minutes later, Uday Kumar, coordinator of the People's Movement Against Nuclear Energy (PMANE), ushers me in, past the outer room where parishioners wait for counselling, into a smaller room, providing introductions and refreshments simultaneously. Apart from parish priest Father Jayakumar and his young assistants, all dressed in white robes, there are others from the PMANE struggle committee—co-founder Pushparyan and associate Muhilan, along with priest-activist Father 'Mahipa' Jesuraj.

An animated discussion on the current political situation in the state—in rapid-fire Tamil—ebbs and flows around me. I drink my tea quietly waiting for Uday's guidance on the logistics of villagers' interviews, local translator, permissions and schedules of PMANE leaders and, most importantly, the women of Idinthakarai.

"This is a small village—approximately 12,000 villagers," he tells me."People are friendly, they will speak freely. You can begin with the women at the Samara *pandal*, or go wherever you want in the village; and you can talk to us in our office anytime," he says, disappearing into his miniscule makeshift office as I finish my 'red' (milk-free) tea.

Geographically speaking, this is a contained and concerted movement. The women of Idinthakarai, who are the principal torch-bearers of the struggle, occupy—in the real and political sense of the word—the Samara *pandal* for a minimum of six hours every day. Their own homes are a stone's throw away, within the village; only one intrepid lady walks the longer distance of 3 km daily from the nearby Tsunami Colony.

The leaders of the movement live in the parish priest's home adjacent to the *pandal*; they have not stepped outside this village since March 2012. If they do, they face immediate arrest in connection with the pending legal cases lodged against them by the Tamil Nadu state government.

The Koodankulam Nuclear Power Plant, or KKNPP, the object of the protestors' ire, is situated less than 2 km away as the crow flies (from the seashore) and less than 5 km according to Nuclear Power Corporation of India (NPCIL) reports. And while six other villages (part of a total of 60-80 supportive villages along the coastline of the three districts of Tirunelveli, Kanyakumari and Tuticorin) are very much at the forefront of the struggle against KKNPP—Koodankulam, Perumanal, Vijaypati, Koottapuli, Varaivikinaru and Koothenkuzhi—Idinthakarai is where it all began. And where it still continues.

The board is simple and stark, mounted on wooden sticks, predominantly white with a red border and a small square in the centre with the number 677 scrawled on it in black chalk. Today is the 677th day of the protest. The date—June 22, 2013—is neatly positioned on the upper right side of the board. In terms of strategy, a board like this serves a dual purpose—it has immediate recall value, reminding everyone, especially visitors, of the continuing suffering and hardship faced by those sitting on such a long protest; *and* it motivates those on the ground, marking off each day as a strike (real and symbolic) against a much more powerful opponent. (American television anchor Walter Cronkite used this power of repetition and recall to great effect during the Iran hostage crisis in 1980, signing off his news bulletin each night by reminding viewers that it was the 300th or 301st day of captivity for the 52 Americans held hostage by Iranian students supporting the Iranian revolution.) Because to be forgotten, to be eclipsed from public memory (unarguably short), to be left to fight alone is the hardest battle of all. Especially when the dice is heavily loaded in your opponent's favour.

Remarkably however, this is not something that perturbs anyone in Idinthakarai.

While the leaders draw parallels with David and Goliath— this is a predominantly Christian community—the women on daily *dharna* (protest) describe it pithily, even humorously: "An ant in the ear of an elephant can cause a lot of trouble, can't it?"

In the entire 'staging area' of the movement—from the vast sandy floors of the *pandal* or temporary shelter covered with a canopy of bamboo sticks, right up to the entrance of the Lourdes church which also contains a small shrine to the martyrs of the movement and numerous posters of nuclear disasters—it is the women of Idinthakarai who dominate and draw you in immediately. They sit in little groups of seven or eight, some knitting, others chatting, the older ones stretched out and sleeping in sunny corners on the sand or on the cool tiles of the vast quadrangle or foyer of the church.

Since there is no fixed time of arrival, there is no head count either; an average of 50 women take part in the daily relay protest.

They finish their household chores, cook for their families, and head towards the protest site every day around 10.30 am. Their next meal will be eaten only after they return home after 4.30 pm.

On this the 677th day of the protest, I approach the first cluster of women sitting around an indigenous board game called *Thaiyyam*—a wooden board with chalk markings, dice, and small pieces of plastic that function as counters—and begin the first of many triangular conversations, with local translator Amal Raj Leon as interpreter. Curiosity weans them away from the game and they are ready to discuss nuclear power and sedition. Other women sidle up to listen and participate, some are obvious leaders deferred to by the rest; the overwhelming majority are involved, interested and articulate.

As I listen to them over the course of the first day (and in the days and months to come), I realise these are no ordinary, uneducated village women sitting in protest because someone—a leader, a husband, a priest—has told them to; they are following the dictates of their individual and collective conscience. They will sit and they will protest and they will endure as long as they need to, armed with nothing more than a unique combination of acquired knowledge and homespun wisdom, a mix that serves them well in the decision-making process.

Snub-nosed and stocky, 38-year-old Sundari is sitting unobtrusively in a corner, speaking on her mobile phone. The transformation into fiery leader, her voice changing, her eyes flashing in righteous anger, is so instantaneous it takes me totally by surprise.

"All we want is that the plant should not be there. The government sets up the plant but if it's not safe it is we who have to face the consequences. Even when we go and buy a TV we get a guarantee, so similarly, why not here? If in the future there is some problem with the plant then who will take care of us? The government does not answer such a basic question. How can we trust that it is safe?" she says, her voice rising.

Before I can react she continues: "We asked them (Nuclear Power Corporation of India, NPCIL, the nodal body that operates all nuclear power plants in the country) what they would do with the (radioactive) waste from the plant. They first said they would let it into the sea; then they said they would bury it. If they let it into the sea, we cannot survive as fishing is our livelihood; if they bury it, the radiation will spread to all the crops and grain, so even agriculture will be affected. And nature is unpredictable; whatever scientists may say, you never know when there could be a disaster like the 2004 tsunami. We are not against producing electricity; we need it, but not in such a way that it destroys people's lives."

Sundari has summed up the position of the protestors in a few, short sentences. The Class 8-educated *beedi* and pickle-maker, mother of two young children, has spent 98 days in jail on 78 charges including sedition. She recites the list nonchalantly: "...Breaking the glass of the police van, making country bombs, talking derogatorily about the chief minister and prime minister, propagating violence, being a traitor to the nation..."

"They told me I have committed a crime against the nation because I am protesting against something which the government has approved. I told them the government was initiated for the people and not the other way around. If they construct something in our homeland then they should ask us first if it is fine with us. The government asked us why we were protesting after 20 years. We said: 'Our parents were not educated but we realise this is not good for us, so we are protesting.' There is no law against protesting. Nobody can tell me not to protest. This is my livelihood; where else will I go? I am not asking the government for food or clothes. I just want them to let me live on my land. I have elected them to power; they should at least let me do that," says Sundari resolutely.

I ask Sundari why she—and so many other women—has chosen the difficult path of protest with no discernible outcome in sight. She does not even have to think about her answer. "People have to live. I am privileged to fight for a cause which will allow people to live. I don't have any fear, I have god with me. Only if you fight you learn about the community. What is the use of sitting at home? I have learnt so much about women, their problems, even when I was in jail. My relatives don't want to mingle with us as they feel my husband has not 'controlled' me. But we still emphasise protest as a method because we want to make sure our children live happy lives. If we struggle now, we can be happy in the future."

In the world according to Sundari, there is an assumed guarantee of deliverance in the future if one works towards a goal in the present. Opposition and roadblocks by government or NPCIL do not dent her optimism. As far as Sundari is concerned, as far as the 50-odd women sitting in protest that day are concerned, all fighting a 'just cause', god is on their side and that is quite enough.

"The Koodankulam nuclear power plant is dangerous and harmful; it hinders our livelihood and causes diseases like tuberculosis, thyroid dysfunction and cancer and that is why we are fighting to shut it down," says 49-year-old Xavier Ammal forcefully. Her voice is perfect for the extensive sloganeering she has done against KKNPP; it is deep, strong and carries its message a long distance. Her personality—and appearance—is equally robust. A thick-set figure, curly greying hair carelessly knotted in a bun, gold-coloured spectacles, gold bangles at the wrists, a gaily patterned synthetic sari, and fingers that deftly make and sort *beedis* from tobacco leaves, Xavier listens to my questions attentively. Her nimble fingers pause only when she begins her reply. Then the words come pouring out; I have to touch her arm to get her to slow down. She is quick to counter-question me, to offer derisive retorts.

Halting this plant (KKNPP) is our only agenda, she tells me earnestly. "We don't want a power plant that threatens our lives; we do need 'current' (electricity) in our state but there are other forms like wind, tidal or solar energy. We don't need it from something that kills people."

Armed with a Class 9 education, Xavier, like most Idinthakarai residents, belies the commonly held perception that village women cannot grasp the intricacies of the nuclear issue.

When I tell her this, she laughs. "We know what we are doing. All the women here read the newspapers. Even the children know what happened in Fukushima, Japan, and they join in our protests against nuclear power. We watch television, we keep ourselves updated. The government thinks we do not know even about electricity. The truth is that in cities like Chennai there are power cuts for perhaps two hours, but here in the villages it is for 14 hours. There are no power cuts in cities so that international corporations can work. The government manipulates the people; the 'current' produced by the plant will be for the large, international companies. They are not going to provide electricity for the villages. We have to pay so that big companies get electricity. Karnataka, Kerala and other states refuse to set up nuclear plants in their states but they want a share of electricity from the Koodankulam plant. Why don't they set up plants in their own states," she asks.

Xavier spent 82 days in prison on sedition charges, in six cases for her role in the September 2012 protestors-police showdown outside the Koodankulam plant. She promises to tell me the story in detail later; it's time for afternoon prayers and Xavier leads the group in paying obeisance to the lord.

The church doors have been opened. The women kneel on the floor outside and pray: a low audible chant in Tamil followed by hymns. Not everyone takes part in this ritual; some women continue chatting, reading, or playing at a distance. No one eats lunch; there is no packed food with the ubiquitous plastic water bottle poking out of handbags and purses. There are no tea breaks either to break the monotony of the protestors' daily routine. Unless there is a specific event scheduled for the day, calling for speeches, sloganeering and crowd-mobilisation, the protest continues silent, steadfast and sedentary.

Any diversions are provided by outsiders—anti-nuke campaigners, journalists of every hue and nationality, students from neighbouring colleges, local politicians on the prowl, and a vast array of activists.

Today Riaas and Anoop, two young mass communication students from a college in Calicut, are filming interviews with the women leaders for a documentary on the Koodankulam plant. I watch Xavier and Sundari speak confidently in front of the camera, explaining their stand, highlighting the key issues of their struggle.

It has been a long and lonely struggle for the most part.

The Koodankulam nuclear power plant was planned as early as 1979 when the Soviet Union initiated a nuclear power deal with the Indian government. The origins of this partnership can be traced back to May 18, 1974 when India detonated a 'peaceful nuclear device' at the Pokhran Test Range in Rajasthan. Having already refused to sign the Nuclear Non-Proliferation Treaty (NPT) in 1968—a pact whereby countries stop the further spread of nuclear weapons—the Pokhran test led to India's isolation from international affairs, especially in the West. The US stopped shipment of fuel to the Tarapur nuclear power plant in Mumbai.

It is against this backdrop, four years after the Bhopal gas tragedy in 1984 and two years after the Chernobyl nuclear disaster in the Soviet Union in 1986, that President Mikhail Gorbachev and Indian Prime Minister Rajiv Gandhi signed an agreement, on November 20, 1988, for two Russian-built nuclear reactors in Koodankulam.

Opposition to the plant began the very next month, with a massive rally in Tirunelveli followed by a protest in Nagercoil in January 1989. In May 1989, around 10,000 protestors assembled under the banner of the National Fish Workers Union, opposing Koodankulam and its proposal to draw water for reactors from the nearby Pechiparai reservoir and to discharge waste water into the sea, threatening the livelihoods of fisherfolk.

Idinthakarai's Mary, who was part of that historic rally, describes the experience: "On May 1, 1989, a mammoth protest was held at Kanyakumari bringing together people from various towns. It was a peaceful, non-violent agitation from the Gandhi *mandapam* on the seashore to the Kanyakumari church. Men, women and children were all part of the protest. But when we were passing through the police station, the police broke the glass panes of buses, got into altercations with us and later blamed us. They beat and shot at us. People from Arockiapuram near Kanyakumari were injured. Pichai and Rex from Idinthakarai were shot in the leg and we admitted them to a Nagercoil hospital. Even after all this we didn't give up. We realised that if we didn't fight, all of Tamil Nadu could be destroyed. So we fought with conviction. At that time there were no news channels and the media did not address the nuclear issue as aggressively as it does today. Later we even protested outside the gates of the plant but the people of Koodankulam village were not with us then. They believed the government's promises of employment for villagers at the time and did not know what the consequences of the plant would be," says Mary.

Villagers claim that when NPCIL acquired approximately 930-1,050 hectares of land (www.infochangeindia.org) for the project, and an additional 150-165 hectares (NPCIL figures) for the township, several promises were made to the local people: of overall development and growth in the region and jobs for the villagers, including a job for one member of every household that sold its land to the government.

On paper and on the ground however no proof exists to verify the claims of promises. But 57-year-old Rajalingam of Koodankulam village remembers: "In 1988, I was part of the RSS (Rashtriya Swayamsevak Sangh, a right-wing Hindu organisation). I later joined the ABVP (Akhil Bharatiya Vidyarthi Parishad, youth wing of the Bharatiya Janata Party) and took part in protests against the plant. NPCIL fooled us by saying that they were setting up industries that would generate employment. My salary was Rs 5 a day at that time, and they told us that we would get Rs 5,000 a month. They left us with dreams of lakhs of rupees in earnings. They got our land virtually free because, lured by the promise of development, we sold our properties at throwaway prices." Many people in Koodankulam village sold their land for as little as Rs 2,000 per acre with paltry compensation for the cashew and tamarind trees on their land, he adds. He brings me a xerox copy of the 'Notice of Award' made out by the land acquisition officer of KKNPP, in May 1993, in the name of 10 people in Koodankulam village for an amount of Rs 2,117 for 0.38 hectares of land acquired.

Since the promised 'industries' turned out to be a nuclear plant and the nature of the work was highly skilled and technical, the jobs on offer for locals were extremely limited. Rajalingam recalls: "People began to feel scared when NPCIL started clearing the whole town—a Roman Catholic school was broken down, and we were sent notices that we could not build new houses in Koodankulam."

With Rajiv Gandhi's assassination and the disintegration of the Soviet Union in 1991, the Koodankulam nuclear project was stalled until, in March 1997, Prime Minister H D Deve Gowda and Russian President Boris Yeltsin signed a supplement to the 1988 agreement.

In 2002, 14 years after the agreement was signed, construction of the Koodankulam nuclear power plant finally began.

The People's Movement Against Nuclear Power (PMANP)—later renamed PMANE—was formed a year earlier. PMANP was a local organisation working in villages near the plant with the single-point agenda of shutting it down. It began raising issues related to the plant's safety and quality and its impact on the region, creating awareness about the consequences of low-level waste and hot water ejected into the sea by the plant, threatening marine life as well as the lives of fishing communities all along the coast.

From the year 2011, the agitation intensified and became more visible with the start of daily sit-in protests and structured planning/strategising by members of a newly-formed 'Struggle Committee'. And struggle they did, on various fronts. Many of their more recent triumphs may indeed be attributed to the movement's survival against all odds.

This June day, 12 years after its inception, PMANE leaders enter the *pandal* for their evening briefing with the women. This is their exclusive time with the women leaders as they update them on the next day or week's agenda, imminent visits by dignitaries, and travel itineraries for women leaders who move outside the village to spread awareness about KKNPP/nuclear issues.

Why did you single out women to be at the forefront of the struggle, I ask Uday as he waits for everyone to gather around for the informal meeting."Because we knew they would not succumb to bribes with money or alcohol," he smiles. "We trusted them to be calm and composed and not fall prey to hatred and animosity. And we have been proved right."

Today's briefing centres around demonstrations to be held the following day over US Secretary of State John Kerry's imminent visit to India and the proposed Indo-US civil nuclear deal. Uday Kumar and Pushparayan sit quietly as Muhilan explains the schedule of events, assigning roles deftly. Several older schoolchildren have by now started trooping in from the higher secondary school nearby, noisily clanging their school bags and water bottles as they spot their mothers in the group. Some venture closer and listen intently. Many will volunteer to join the protest tomorrow—as they have done in the past—since it is not a school day.

Others troop home on their own, knowing their mothers will follow once their day's work at the *pandal* is done. It is a familiar ritual, one they have accepted as the norm a long time ago.

"Venda, venda anu ulai venda! (We don't want nuclear power)" shouts a young boy on his way out, grinning mischievously. The assembly breaks into spontaneous laughter. As the old Tamil saying goes: '*Vilayum payir mulaiyilaeyae theriyum*' (the traits of a sapling can be seen in the seed).

Chapter Two

A Nuclear Plant In Your Backyard

"Venda venda anu ulai venda...America venda!" (We don't want nuclear power, we don't want America), the childish voice rises rhythmically and confidently over the microphone, accompanied by a chorus of six schoolgirls dressed in their Sunday best. The children, none older than 13, are at a demonstration on June 23, 2013, against US Secretary of State John Kerry's visit to India. They also rail against upcoming nuclear plants at Kovvada in Andhra Pradesh and Mithi Virdi in Gujarat, protesting that nuclear power will destroy the country. Standing in front of a microphone in the church foyer, framed by the women, children and leaders of Idinthakarai, their young voices coax willing responses and encouraging smiles from those seated behind them. The front rows are a colourful blend of little children with flowers in their hair, incongruously waving black flags, while the movement's leaders sit inconspicuously at the back, content to wait their turn.

It is mid-morning and the children's chorus is a preface to the speeches that follow. Muhilan and Uday Kumar speak passionately to a crowd of 200-odd 'project-affected persons' or PAP.

"We have been asking NPCIL so many questions about the Koodankulam plant through RTI (right to information) but they keep sending us from one government department to another. They use delaying tactics; they know something is wrong and they are trying to hide the truth from us. But that is like hiding a large pumpkin under a heap of rice! Our two-year struggle has uncovered the truth," declares Uday onstage, his simile drawing amused smiles from the women.

(The RTI queries he refers to addressed a wide range of issues from the Emergency Preparedness Plan to charges of 'faulty' components from a Russian company used at the plant. In most of the cases, according to Uday, responses from AERB/NPCIL were dilatory and dismissive.)

Once the speeches are over, the protest shifts to the street outside, opposite the parish priest's residence. The indefatigable Muhilan leads the demonstrators, holding black flags and placards proclaiming: 'Enemy of the Human Race, Minister of America John Kerry, Go Back; Do Not Enter Our Country' in Tamil. His strenuous anti-nuclear chants receive lively backing from priest Mahipa who, today, is not dressed in his customary white robes. The crowd responds. The demonstration is captured live by local Tamil news cameras that seem to have materialised from nowhere.

Uday Kumar gives a sombre interview to the Tamil news channels, citing the 1984 Bhopal gas tragedy as a precedent for the way governments allow the guilty, like Union Carbide chairman Warren Anderson, to get away with impunity whilst affording the victims little justice. He slams the proposed Indo-US deal to change India's Civil Liability for Nuclear Damage (CLND) Act 2010, allowing suppliers (like US companies) to sidestep liability for any accident that may occur in a nuclear reactor supplied by them.

A quartet of bikers who have driven down from neighbouring Kerala to express their solidarity rev their machines and ride off in an adrenaline-pumping storm. As the heat and dust settle, the crowd begins to disperse. The leaders go back into their houses and the women in the *pandal* wind up their 678th day of protest and head home. Tomorrow, life will return to normal and there will be no spotlight on their activities, their lives, their problems. Until another major event in Koodankulam grabs the attention of the country and the world.

But what is an 'ordinary' day, month, year in the life of people who live 1, 2 or 3 km from a nuclear power plant expected to go critical in less than 30 days?

I begin an exploratory journey through Idinthakarai's narrow lanes and colourful homes painted vivid shades of pink, magenta, blue, purple and green. A few short steps away from the protest *pandal* I am at the seashore. In the absence of a sandy beach there is a T-shaped bulwark of stones one can step across to reach a vantage point at the very end. Looming over the remote village are the twin white-and-ochre domes of KKNPP. I recall the taxi driver slowing to point them out during my ride into Idinthakarai; the plant was at a considerable distance but it was a landmark he felt compelled to show me, adding in broken English: "Nobody is permitted to go inside."

Walking past a line of bright blue, long boats neatly positioned at the water's edge in front of the fishermen's huts, I watch a group of men mending their nets. When I finally summon up the courage to disturb them, 49-year-old Britto obliges me first, his matter-of-fact narrative reflecting stoic acceptance of a life full of uncertainties and limited options.

"I drink rice water and go fishing early in the morning. Since we fishermen are engrossed in our work, which is extremely difficult, we don't feel hungry. We eat when we return home which could be 5 or 6 in the evening. If we go fishing at night we may eat a little, but generally we have our meals only when we return the next morning at 8. When the sea is rough it is difficult to cast our nets, so it is a tough life. But it is the only life we know. We don't have any other skills, our lives depend on fishing. That is why whenever we have time we join in the protests against the plant," says Britto earnestly.

Fishermen constitute a majority (approximately 70%, according to PMANE) of the working population of the coastal villages that are actively protesting the plant. Tirunelveli district, where Koodankulam and Idinthakarai are located, has approximately 23,000 fishermen going out to sea every day, from seven villages along its 48km coastline. Other occupations in the district include agriculture, animal husbandry, brick-making and small industries. In Idinthakarai, the average monthly income of a family (the women roll *beedis* and make pickle) is Rs 15,000-20,000, sometimes more if there's a good catch, says translator Amal Raj. Climate and the seasons determine the market rate of fish, he adds. During the 'no fishing' season (the months of June, July and August) the rates are much higher; a fish poacher could earn Rs 400 a day selling his catch.

Every family in Idinthakarai contributes a tenth of its earnings each week to the collection box that sustains the people's movement against KKNPP. Britto says his catch and therefore his earnings vary from Rs 500-1,000 a day—and sometimes nothing at all. He doesn't own a boat but informs me that a fibre one could cost as much as Rs 1-3 lakh; boat engines cost Rs 1 lakh and nets around Rs 50,000.

I ask him what kind of a life he envisages for his four children, and whether or not KKNPP figures in it. He waves his arms vigorously in the negative. "The plant will not let us live. It will cause diseases with its radiation. We will not be able to fish either, as the fish will be killed by the radiation in the water. No one will want such fish in any case. Then what will become of us?"

Britto informs me that he was part of the first people's protest against the plant in 1989, in Kanyakumari, and was beaten by the police.

He tells me about the time Idinthakarai villagers read notices in the Kanyakumari district edition of *Dinakaran* newspaper, providing safety instructions during the plant's trial runs in August 2011. "That alerted us to the danger and we began our protests in a big way."

Britto is proud of his wife who is part of the daily protest group at the Samara *pandal*. He is also grateful for the leadership of Uday Kumar and other PMANE leaders. "We called Uday Kumar because we are not educated and feared that the government may cheat us," he says frankly.

Did anyone from the government come here and talk to the villagers about the plant? Nobody came and nobody spoke to us, he says simply. Would the people of Idinthakarai accept anything short of the plant's closure? Would they have relocated, if asked? "We will never relocate because this is our land," says Britto emphatically. "Moreover, we need the sea to survive. The plant should be closed down. People who live in the cities do not know the issues here even though they are educated. We are the ones who slog it out every day, and only we know what is involved." Ultimately, in the 'unequal fight' between the powerful government and the villagers, Britto adds, "all we can do is ask for the plant to be scrapped; if we get no response we can trust only god to help us".

The other fishermen working nearby have by now gathered up their nets and are calling out to Britto to head on home with the day's catch.

Walking past several houses built abutting each other in what appears to be a riotously colourful competition—pink, blue, purple, magenta, red, orange—I pause to watch a determined group of eight-or nine-year-old boys trying to chase and then sit inside an old rubber tyre turn by turn while the rest cheer from the shade of a spreading banyan tree. It is a gentle flashback to a simpler life in a simpler time.

Gnanaprakasam, 82, unshaven with wisps of white, uncombed hair framing his wizened features, is a relic of just such a time in Idinthakarai. A time when fishermen like him chased shoals of fish for days, based on just wind patterns and the changing seasons. They would row the boats themselves and had no concept of time—when they spotted fish, they chased, bagged and sold it.

"People were nice in those days, now their character has changed. Foodgrain used to be pure and fresh and I could eat a lot; now I cannot since it costs much more," says the old man. He doesn't quite have the stomach for food these days either.

Gnanaprakasam has lived in this village all his life and remembers resting in the area where NPCIL later set up KKNPP: "We used to go rabbit-hunting and rest on that land. Later, people came to measure it. We didn't know then that there was anything dangerous about what they were doing." He only learnt about the potential danger of the plant three years ago. In September 2012 he took part in the mass protest and was severely injured in the ensuing police *lathi*-charge.

His testimony is recorded in a fact-finding report on the incidents of September 10 and 11, 2012, submitted by senior journalist Kalpana Sharma, former judge of the Bombay High Court B G Kolse Patil and Joe D'Cruz, a Chennai-based writer:

> *Gnanaprakasam, who claims to be more than 100 years old, and who could barely walk, showed us the deep wound on the back of his head, which had been stitched. He said that he was brutally attacked by police even though he had no capacity to be violent and also because he did not believe in violence. "We are asking serious questions and we want answers and we don't think violence is a means in this debate. But violence is what we got in response," he said.*

I ask him why he went for the protests given his age and frail health. He looks at me in surprise: "Of course I had to go. My elder brother is ill so he can't go. If I also don't go, how will it look? I was brought up here and my children live here. This is my land; it is my duty to go. And why should I be scared? I don't fear death; even if the world ends I don't fear death. The plant should be closed down, that's all. If we all stand united, we can do it," he says forcefully. His wife nods in agreement. She participated in the sit-in of 2012 and still attends all major PMANE events.

Unity is taken for granted in Idinthakarai—it has been for the past 678 days at least—as the protests move forward at a pace dictated either by unfolding events or advance planning by the movement's leaders. Virtually every house in the village supports the women sitting in the *pandal* every day. Those who can spare time join in whenever possible; the men attend village council meetings with PMANE leaders to deliberate all major decisions involving the village; the children are pressed into willing service as cheerleaders and a youthful vanguard at key events.

In a tiny house a few lanes from the *pandal*, Gracepin (8), Grashini (9), and Grasiha (4) break into Tamil anti-nuclear songs effortlessly and on cue. The song they are singing—roughly translated—goes like this: "Close down the nuclear plant in Koodankulam, send it in a coffin all the way to Russia!" As the singing session ends, they look to the adults for approval and receive it in abundance from me, translator Amal Raj and their grandmother Mary. Cherubic Grashini is older, but Gracepin is the more talkative: "I study in the second standard and I know that a nuclear plant causes radiation which causes diseases like tuberculosis, thyroid disorders and cancer in women. Everybody in the village, including my grandmother, is protesting to shut the plant." His sister pitches in shyly: "I don't want the nuclear plant because children can be born deformed, women may be rendered childless, and people may die also. Whenever I have a holiday from school I too go to protest." The youngest sibling, four-year-old Grasiha, refuses to be cajoled into speaking, preferring to trail her mother Kalaiveni who is making tea in the kitchen.

Thirty-two-year-old Kalaiveni is a near-perfect example of an aspirational bridge between two generations—her mother Mary rolled *beedis* (earning as little as Rs 7 for 100 *beedis* at one time; she now earns Rs 100-150 a week) to put her through 12th grade and a nursing diploma. Mary's husband died at sea when her daughter was a baby. Kalaiveni hopes her own children become doctors and engineers some day; their father earns a meagre salary in Dubai at a fibre factory, while she works as a nursing aide at the village hospital.

In the hurly-burly of life and the struggle to keep an even keel and earn a decent living, the shadow of the Koodankulam nuclear plant is constant and inescapable. The community has a deep and long-term commitment to preserving the safety of their land and people. "I have lived here all my life," says Kalaiveni. "I want my children and future generations to live here peacefully without any harm...We will fight till the plant is stopped. I am proud of my mother for going to protest every day despite her ill health; she is fighting for the next generation," she says emotionally.

Mary, who has just returned from the day's sit-in and has been quietly drinking her tea, now joins in with her experiences of over two decades. The sitting room of her small house is cluttered with schoolbags strewn on the lone steel bed. A tiny badminton racquet and toys flung about on a table nearby signal the daily routine of small children. For the moment, however, as their grandmother talks of serious matters, they play in the open courtyard outside the kitchen where a few plants vie for space along with several colourful plastic water containers. The house is spotlessly clean, steel utensils shining in the kitchen in neatly propped rows, floors all dusted and swept.

"My house is approximately 1.5 km away from the Koodankulam plant," begins Mary.

I ask if she is aware of the Atomic Energy Regulatory Board (AERB) guidelines that specify no habitation/population at all within the exclusion zone comprising a 1.6-km radius around the plant, less than 20,000 people in the 5-km radius of the sterilisation zone, and 100,000 people within 30 km—all of which have been violated/infringed in the case of the Koodankulam plant.

No, she says in a familiar refrain, nobody told us anything. "No one came here to tell us that they would protect us or rehabilitate or help us if there was any disaster related to the plant; neither did they invite us anywhere to explain anything. When the Fukushima disaster occurred in Japan, only then people here became aware of the dangers and the media took notice of the issue."

On March 11, 2011, the Fukushima Daiichi nuclear plant in Japan was hit by a 15-metre tsunami triggered by a major earthquake, resulting in the meltdown of three of six nuclear reactors, with substantial amounts of radioactive materials released into the air and water. The nuclear accident was rated level 7 on the INES (International Nuclear and Radiological Events Scale), the highest level, denoting a major accident.

Physicians for Social Responsibility (PSR), a US-based physician-led organisation against nuclear proliferation, estimated: "Radioactive cesium has taken up residence in the (Fukushima) exclusion zone, replacing the human inhabitants. Cesium-137 has a half-life of 30 years, and since it takes about 10 half-lives for any radionuclide to disappear, it will maintain ownership of the exclusion zone for centuries."

The Japanese Science Ministry reported (in November 2011) that long-lived radioactive cesium had contaminated 30,000 km of the country's land space.

The human cost of the Fukushima disaster will not be known for years. Cancer as a result of radiation exposure can occur decades later. Official records compiled by the Fukushima Prefecture mention 1,607 deaths directly tied to disaster-related injuries, and 1,656 deaths related to stress and other illnesses. Approximately 160,000 people were evicted from the exclusion zones, losing their home and possessions, living as evacuees, not knowing if they could ever return.

Once images of the Fukushima disaster flooded the television screens of Mary and those living in close proximity to the Koodankulam plant, government guarantees of safety could do little to dispel the fear that this could, someday, be their fate too. Visuals of Fukushima's devastation, evacuation, panic, and government disarray shook the residents of Idinthakarai, Tsunami Colony, Koodankulam, Vairavikinaru, Vijaypathi, Koothakuzhi, Kootapuli and other villages along the coast. It spurred them to immediate action. This was the first trigger of the people's struggle against KKNPP.

The one thought on everyone's mind was—how might the Indian government have reacted had this disaster happened next door in Koodankulam? The government's track record in disaster management during natural calamities such as the tsunami (2004), Orissa cyclone (1999), earthquakes in Latur (1993) and Gujarat (2001), and floods of varying intensity across the country did not inspire much confidence.

Their apprehension was not unfounded. A CAG report on the functioning of the National Disaster Management Authority (NDMA) revealed that this nodal body in charge of disasters nationwide had no working plan seven years after it was set up; its National Risk Mitigation Project had barely progressed five years after conceptualisation; and its Response Fund was diverted to uses other than disaster management. NDMA guidelines are the ones to be followed by NPCIL, the state and district administrations in case of a disaster at the Koodankulam plant.

In a rare moment of candour, S A Bhardwaj, director technical, NPCIL, admitted at a press conference in March 2012:

"Even nuclear experts were shaken by the Fukushima disaster. So if the general public or locals are asking questions, their concerns are genuine and we have to address them."

Public concerns were addressed by AERB speedily setting up a taskforce in March 2011 to conduct a 'Safety Evaluation of Indian Nuclear Power Plants post-Fukushima Incident'. The taskforce was tasked with suggesting improvements in reactor safety. Its final report in August 2011 recommended 17 safety measures specifically for the Koodankulam plant, complete with timelines for implementation, which were accepted by NPCIL.

On July 1, 2011, NPCIL announced the start of the 'hot run' phase of the first reactor, a month-long process, as recorded by NPCIL, involving testing and venting of steam relief valves. The hot run caused a great deal of noise and smoke. This was the second trigger for alarm; worried villagers now had tangible signs of how their lives may be impacted. No one had any information about how long the operation would last, how much smoke or noise would continue to be emitted, and how they were to handle its effects.

The information that was provided to PAP (project-affected people) the very next month (August 2011) proved to be the third trigger for the people's movement. It came in the form of a 'mock drill' advisory published by NPCIL, on August 8, 2011, in the Nagercoil edition of *Dinakaran*, a Tamil newspaper.

Mary recalls the procedures they were advised to follow in case of a disaster. Translated from the Tamil, they read:

Things to do during an emergency:

1. Cover your face and mouth with a cloth, handkerchief or towel, and proceed to the nearest house or building.

Switch off the air-conditioner in the building/house and close the windows and doors of the house.

2. Switch on the TV or radio and follow the instructions given through it. Follow the suggestions given by the district and regional medical authorities and take the iodine tablets as instructed.

3. Do not leave the house or building in which you are staying, unless you are instructed by the district authorities to do so.

Things to avoid during an emergency:

1. Do not become panicky and spread rumours. Do not act on rumours.

2. Do not leave the place you are staying in without any announcement. Do not roam around in open areas.

3. Do not eat food from vessels which are not covered.

The notice set off alarm bells in more ways than one, according to Mary. "Many villagers realised that there might be real cause for worry and they joined in the protests. We fought harder, concerned not only about ourselves but about all of Tamil Nadu which could be impacted by the plant."

Activists from the Madras Atomic Power Plant or MAPS at Kalpakkam (665 kilometers away from KKNPP)visited, told them about the effects of radiation on health, and shared stories of accidents and deaths related to nuclear radiation at the nuclear plant there. This further spurred the villagers into protesting, says Mary frankly.

Mary has been sitting in at the daily protest for 678 days, and has participated in five hunger strikes including a week-long fast which led to her hospitalisation. Where does she get the will to carry on despite her weak back and ill health? Her answer is predictable: "God gives us the strength to fight; we must save our land and our people."

People say we are being paid to protest, she adds, dismissing the most damning and frequent criticism against the women's agitation. "But we haven't taken a single rupee from anyone. We keep aside a tenth of our income for this cause, for costs such as putting up tents or maintaining the *pandal*. Sometimes people come and donate money, but we don't take money from any other country. We take pride in looking after people who come from abroad, we don't take money from them."

I tell her about rumours of daily payments of Rs 300 to protestors, allegations of 'foreign funding', sneers of 'biryani sit-ins', and her response is characteristically stoic: "People who want to insult us and fling mud at us say things like that. They say we will leave all this and run away one day. No matter how much they insult us, we will not stop protesting because the sea is our livelihood, we can only survive here. Everyone is fighting—not just us fisherfolk but also the farmers and labourers—disregarding all barriers of caste and religion."

But how long can they sustain this movement, especially in the face of a government disinclined to listen to dissenting voices in a far-flung corner of the country? Mary's answer reflects the stand of all the supporters of the struggle against KKNPP: their fight is a just one and will continue till the plant is shut down. "There's no going back; we will fight till we emerge victorious. The authorities claim that people die even in bus or plane accidents. But the casualties there are limited to 50 or 60. In a nuclear accident, unborn generations will also suffer."

Perhaps there was less awareness when they began, Mary concedes, but now the community supports them, the media sees their pain and highlights their protest. Translator Amal Raj adds: "Idinthakarai was mentioned at a Fukushimaprotest rally of 60,000 people in Japan—MDMK (Marumalarchi Dravida Munetra Kazhagam) leader Vaiko told us this. So people do know about us!"

As her daughter Kalaiveni brings in refreshments for a tea break, Mary watches her grandchildren eat their biscuits and practise their English with me. Her indulgent expression turns serious and she says: "Radiation from the plant can affect our children, but the worst-affected will be women who can have miscarriages or abortions or deformed children. Radiation can also lead to impotency in men. If we know there is a snake in a hole, will we put our hand inside? The nuclear plant is a huge snake and we know it is fatal, so how can we leave without killing it?" Mary has her own brand of homespun logic.

It's the women who spearhead the daily protests, Mary explains, because the men must go out to fish. They mark their presence only at major protests. "Fish do not stay in one place, they don't come with a label saying 'Idinthakarai fish' or 'Kanyakumari fish'—all fish will carry the radiation so everybody will be affected. This is why people elsewhere will also support our fight," she says confidently. Apart from the five coastal villages closest to the plant and two in the interior—Koottapuli, Perumanal, Kootenkuzhi, Koodankulam, Vairavikinaru, Thomayarpuram and Uvari—PMANE claims as many as 60-80 coastal villages in Kanyakumari, Tirunelveli and Tuticorin districts support the anti-KKNPP movement.

Mary is 57 years old. She has been part of the protests against

KKNPP since 1988 and vows to continue as long as she lives. She laments the transformation of the plant site from the fertile fields of paddy and tamarind trees she played in as a teenager, to a desert. This is not the world she wants for her children. "Health problems such as fever are common and we have to deal with them. But now we have to worry about life-threatening diseases such as cancer, tuberculosis, thyroid disorders, or deformities as a result of radiation. My life is getting over but we want our future generations to have a good life on this land."

Another early morning, another foray into the colourful dwellings of Idinthakarai village, past fresh fish being sold by a mother-daughter duo in the open courtyard of their home, the fish spread out on a straw pallet held down by stones at opposite ends. The intentionally meandering walk is interspersed with brief chats with curious villagers more than willing to explain their point of view. From the last house at the very end of the lane all one can see is a large canvas of open, green land dotted with trees. And a little beyond, the twin domes of KKNPP: less than a kilometre from the terrace of the house I am standing in that morning, talking to the owner.

We fisherfolk don't want that plant, the middle-aged lady with windblown hair says vociferously, pointing to it rather unnecessarily. Shut it down, she adds.

Down a dusty red road snaking its way roughly 1.5 km to Tsunami Colony, flanked by greenery on all sides and bizarre windmills at regular intervals, an old man walks his bicycle with his grandson trotting alongside. The rest of the way, the wind, the windmills and the bright blue sky are my only companions. A black marble foundation stone marks the entrance to Tsunami Colony, the names of NGO donors and government officials etched on it for posterity. The 450 houses here were in fact built by CASA (Church's Auxiliary for Social Action) and handed over to rehabilitated villagers in 2006, two years after the Boxing Day tsunami of December 26, 2004.

The 9.3 Richter scale earthquake off the coast of Sumatra, followed by the tsunami in the Indian Ocean, caused untold loss of life, property and livelihoods in coastal India. The government (Ministry of Home Affairs report, May 25, 2005) reported the "deaths of 12,405 persons, with 5,640 missing and 647,599 displaced from their homes; across the entire Indian coast that was affected by the tsunami an estimated 1,089 villages were affected, 157,393 houses destroyed, approximately 730,000 forced to leave their homes, 83,788 boats damaged or destroyed, 31,755 livestock lost, and 39,035 hectares of ripe, agricultural land damaged".

Tamil Nadu's 1,076-km coastline witnessed massive destruction: more than 10 lakh people were directly or indirectly impacted as the waves engulfed several coastal districts, causing at least 8,000 people to lose their lives, flattening 230 villages and 418 hamlets across 13 coastal districts and rendering thousands homeless. Fisher communities along the coast whose survival depends on the sea were the main victims of the killer waves that reshaped the coastline. No systems were in place to provide timely warnings for emergency evacuation.

In Tirunelveli district—where Idinthakarai, Koodankulam, Vairavikinaru and other PAP villages are situated—13 hamlets were affected, and 5,626 families found to be in the high tide risk zone advised to relocate to safer places.

Tsunami Colony was built by CASA on land provided by the government. The KKNPP plant, which began construction in 2002, is just 2 km from the rehabilitation site. This puts the entire colony in violation of AERB's exclusion zone specifying 'no habitation within a 1.5-km radius from the plant'. The rehabilitation colony was inaugurated in November 2006.

I enter the colony of houses laid out neatly in parallel lanes, rather like the well-arranged boxes on a Monopoly board, with random trees providing green relief, and am trailed by a silent, thin young boy. He escorts me around, speaking in halting English and rapid-fire Tamil. As self-appointed guide, he accommodates my request for an overview of the area and takes me to the only two-storey terraced house from where I am able to see the colony spread out in front of me, the domes of KKNPP half-a-kilometre behind me.

Thirteen-year-old Ignatius, a Class 7 student, has attended every protest against the nuclear plant that is so close to his home. He rattles off information that has been shared with him by adults like a seasoned campaigner. "Every day when they (NPCIL) started the reactor (during the trial runs), it made loud noises, making babies and small children cry. Young children would come running home thinking the reactor had been switched on and scared they would be affected in some way. During the prawn-fishing season, our fishermen are threatened and forced to steer away from the best fishing sites by the plant people. When we were rehabilitated to this colony after the tsunami snatched away our homes, we were not aware of the reactor, the radiation and the consequences."

Ignatius sounds years older than his age. I ask him whether he thinks he has grown up too quickly because of the nuclear plant, and whether he has missed out on his childhood. He doesn't quite comprehend the question and replies tangentially: "The government, the chief minister...they don't care about us.

They should have helped children like us at least, but they don't treat us well. They are not letting us live in peace. We protest on the seashore because we have to survive here. If they don't let us live on our own land, where will we go? That is why we protest."

"Nobody called me to agitate, it was my decision," he informs me importantly. "I listened to speeches people made, I learnt from them and then I myself gave speeches onstage. We children also devise slogans and chant them to unite people for the cause. We want to protect not just ourselves but future generations, making sure babies are born healthy, not deformed as a result of radiation from the plant, babies that evoke pity. Since nobody supports us, we have to fight for ourselves and make sure India progresses," Ignatius ends passionately.

Children are judiciously woven into the protest framework of the PMANE strategy, frontlining demonstrations sometimes, adding to crowd presence at other times, but always a reliable force that leaders and protesting women can count on to bolster flagging energies or dwindling numbers. And whether it is little children aged four or five lustily shouting the *anu-ulai venda* (we don't want nuclear power) slogans, or older ones reciting poems, writing protest letters or making fiery speeches to an appreciative audience, the level of awareness about this complex issue is extraordinary.

Tsunami Colony resident and a Class 10 student, 14-year-old Luvsana is perhaps their most confident youth spokesperson, making cogent arguments before not just the media but also the Tirunelveli collector! Luvsana belongs to a large family of six sisters and two brothers, ranging from age two to 20. Her mother Tamilarasi, a *beedi* worker, is the only resident of Tsunami Colony who trudges the 3-km distance to and from the protest *pandal* at

Idinthakarai every day. The others in the colony attend only the main protest events.

Luvsana had accompanied Mary to the collector's office to submit a petition demanding that NPCIL comply with the 17 safety conditions listed by the AERB-appointed taskforce post-Fukushima before commissioning the plant.

Dressed in the regulation brown school uniform, hair in two neat ribboned pigtails, Luvsana describes her encounter with the collector with scorn: "We had gone to the collector's office on a holiday. He didn't even know it was a holiday and asked me why I wasn't in school. We didn't get a chance to talk for even five minutes. We told him we are against nuclear power when he asked us why we had come with the petition, but he was more interested in getting us out of there. Mary Aunty and I were the only ones who spoke to him, no one else was allowed in. We told him to take the issue seriously as we have to survive on this land; we are fighting for our lives. I was telling him how the plant is unsafe because of the poor quality of materials used when the media came in and the collector got worried that they would hear what I was saying. So he called the police and hustled us out.

"He advised me to concentrate on my studies instead of talking about nuclear power; I told him I have to be alive to concentrate on my studies!" chuckles Luvsana, her eyes twinkling." Only if the nuclear plant is shut down will I remain alive to study and become a collector like him."

Luvsana, who wants to study for the IPS exams, has read up on the Chernobyl and Fukushima disasters and extrapolates that KKNPP could meet a similar fate. "I am not illiterate. The Chernobyl and Fukushima plants were supposed to be safe but they burst. What if KKNPP bursts too? Who will look after us then? We have been protesting for the last two-and-a-half years but the government ignores us. When they want votes they come to us, after that nothing happens. And they never give information about the dangers of the plant and how harmful it is," she says animatedly.

Luvsana attends the Bishop Roche Higher Secondary School in Idinthakarai. The village also has two primary schools for boys and girls. Tirunelveli district and Kanyakumari district, where pockets of support for the movement exist among coastal villages, have fairly high literacy levels at 79% and 90% respectively. The sex ratio in both districts is 1,025 and 1,019 females per 1,000 males, higher than the national average of 940 females per 1,000 males (Census 2011).

Tamilarasi watches Luvsana with justifiable pride. She and her husband Sahayaraj are illiterate and want to give all their eight children (six daughters and two sons) the best possible education. And a future without a nuclear plant operating in their backyard. To this end, Tamilarasi cooks for her family early in the morning, picks up her two-year-old toddler, walks 3 km to Idinthakarai, sits with the women at the *pandal* from 11 am onwards, and walks back at 5 pm. She is at the vanguard of the movement, always curious, always involved, a permanent smile on her thin, unadorned face.

Her small house—Number 377 in Tsunami Colony—is cluttered with random toys, a television, a broken transistor, two large teddy bears, and odd pots and pans. As one daughter covers her school books and the youngest toddler runs around the room looking for her clothes, Tamilarasi brings out a gigantic poster of MGR, former Tamil Nadu chief minister and film superstar. They don't make politicians like him anymore she laughs, adding that

MGR's protégé Jayalalitha may have done some good initially but had proved disappointing in the end.

I ask her if anyone from the government has visited Tsunami Colony or talked about disaster management or an evacuation plan in case of an emergency. She shakes her head. "Nobody tells us anything. We live half-a-kilometre away from the plant, we observe it, we see that it is not in good shape. The government lies to us that the plant is safe so we have to protest against it, otherwise they will not stop. When they conduct trial runs at the plant, the sound is so loud that my children are terrified and tell me we should all run away as the plant is going to burst. At the end of the trial runs, black-and-white smoke is released; it makes our throats hurt and eyes burn. The sound continues incessantly for five or six days, so loud that our houses vibrate."

This is the second time the residents of Tsunami Colony are grappling with an uncertain future and a dangerous present, says Tamilarasi. The first was when the 2004 tsunami swept away their homes and belongings. "I lost my house and only managed to find a cupboard and a bed," she says sadly. No one seems to have offered the residents of Tsunami Colony the option of resettling in any area other than this one with a nuclear plant within a kilometre of it. "In Idinthakarai, where our homes were swept away, there was a danger of the tsunami recurring, and here there is the nuclear plant, so we would be safe neither here nor there. We had no option really," says Tamilarasi.

Thirty-four-year-old Rani Kervin lives in one of the houses closest to the plant. Her two youngest children, hanging like monkeys from a tree just outside their home, point it out. Rani admits to "feeling worried all the time", partly due to the trauma endured (and anticipated in the future) during trial runs at the plant. She describes the relentless sound and "black smoke that causes suffocation" when the family is forced to shut all doors and windows and huddle inside while the whole house vibrates.

The hot run trials lasted all of July 2011, fuelling the anxieties of people who were not forewarned about the smoke and the sound. After the trials, conducted at KKNPP, Swapnesh Malhotra, head of the DAE's public awareness division, admitted in an online interview: "When the valves are opened (during the hot run) there is a loud shrieking sound. Imagine a thousand pressure-cookers blowing their whistles at the same time; anyone would be petrified. We did not communicate this to the locals."

Though she has studied till Class 12, Rani became aware of the 'dangers' of living next to a nuclear plant only in 2004 when she heard people discussing the issue, during a visit to Radhapuram for a birth certificate for her child. "Today everyone knows the dangers. People fell ill because of the sound and smoke; we got fever, dysentery and vomiting," she tells me earnestly. Did you tell the authorities about it, I ask her."No, we did not, because nobody cares about us. No one fights for us, we feel alone. We just bought the medicines (potassium iodate tablets to combat radiation as prescribed in the NPCIL advisory)," is her dejected reply.

You have already lost a house in the 2004 tsunami; what do you fear losing now, I ask. "We don't know if we will survive at all," says Rani frankly, "but how can we leave the land we were born and brought up on? I have lived here for 34 years. We need the sea to survive. Moreover, the NPCIL guards do not let our fishermen catch prawns near the plant area, so how are we supposed to earn our livelihood," she asks angrily.

What does she base her hopes for a better future for her three young children on, I ask.

"I send them to English-medium schools, and I know the plant will close down because the corrupt government has not used good materials. And of course we have immense faith in god and our protests. The tears of the people will not spare them (government/KKNPP)," declares Rani, her eyes shining brightly.

As young Ignatius guides me out of Tsunami Colony against the backdrop of a spectacular sunset and the flashing lights of the twin domes of KKNPP, I recall what PMANE leader Uday Kumar had said to me that morning: "To keep hope alive in difficult times, to be positive, to sound positive is very important."

As a mantra for life or a motivational tool, it seems to be a lesson well learnt by the people of Idinthakarai in their fight against a formidable opponent.

Chapter Three

LIVING IN EXILE: LEADERS OF A LONELY MOVEMENT

"Uday Kumar is a terrorist...don't travel in a vehicle arranged by him, it will be shadowed by the Tamil Nadu police." The words hissed over the telephone are a warning from a well-meaning Madurai-based acquaintance on hearing about my journey to Idinthakarai.

At the Koodankulam police station, Uday Kumar is officially listed as 'Accused Number 1' in as many as 380 cases—on charges of 'sedition', 'waging war against the state', even 'attempt to murder'. He and his associates on the PMANE struggle committee are routinely vilified—by sections of the media, by fellow Tamilians and pro-nuclear groups, by political parties, and by the government of course—for accepting 'foreign funding' and leading a 'sponsored agitation'.

The common perception among people in a state desperate to resolve its power paucity issues (Tamil Nadu has electricity cuts lasting up to 10 hours a day even in cities, barring capital city Chennai) is that the 'foreign-funded' PMANE agitation is a major obstacle on the road to abundant power supply once

KKNPP is operational.

None of the criticism bothers the quiet, soft-spoken man working in his miniscule office in the parish priest's residence. Though high-ceilinged, the austere, even shabby room is an incredibly cramped space, barely large enough to accommodate two ordinary desks with computers connected by a tangled mass of thick black wires, and sundry books, papers, old newspapers, water bottles and cheap wall calendars.

Dr S P Uday Kumar, 53, dressed in his trademark white *veshti* (traditional South Indian attire) and shirt, has a wide infectious smile and often uses ironic humour to deflect the grimness of the situation he deals with on a daily basis. Isn't this the classic David versus Goliath fight, I ask him, where anti-nuclear power protests manage to make a lot of noise and get media coverage but eventually fail to stop the actual functioning of the plant?

"We are no match for the huge and powerful Indian state," admits Uday with a smile. "When I talk to the group I often invoke the analogy of a drunken male chauvinist husband and a poor housewife who is regularly beaten up by him. She cannot obviously build her muscles to match his physical strength and fight him. All she can use is her moral strength to point out his tyranny to neighbours and others and refuse to cooperate with him. That is exactly what we can and are doing."

Have they succeeded?

"I think we have. Maybe we haven't physically locked the plant and taken away the key. But we have managed to halt it and prove categorically that their claims of 100% safety are wrong, that Dr Abdul Kalam (former President of India and a staunch advocate of nuclear power) is wrong. Moreover, even if they do manage to crush us, the impact of our struggle on successive generations will be quite powerful. They may hide these things and bring other equipment and components to make it run in the next year or so. But we have sowed the seeds of distrust and suspicion in the minds of millions of people," says Uday emphatically.

The goal was always to shut down the Koodankulam plant, he admits frankly; it was a single-point agenda. "When we started the People's Movement Against Nuclear Energy in 2001, this was foremost in our minds. Whenever and wherever we went, we talked about the project, saying it was not good. Of course it was not only based on the NIMBY (not-in-my-back-yard) factor; we also said that nuclear energy is not good and we should get rid of it, not only in India or South Asia but in the whole world. So we are starting with our neighbourhood, our backyard, and Koodankulam has to be scrapped. That has remained our consistent demand," affirms Uday.

The strategy devised was multifold—agitational, legal, environmental and informational—each strategy managed by people with appropriate skill sets. There were scientists, engineers, doctors and advocates who helped take decisions and also interacted with the government. In some cases, fees such as legal fees for court hearings were waived by senior advocates such as Prashant Bhushan who fought for their cause. G Sundar Rajan, member of environmental activist organisation Poovulagin Nanbargal or Friends of Earth (not connected with the international organisation by that name) and coordinator of PMANE's technical team along with Dr Pugazhendhi and Dr V T Padmanabhan, explains the clear division of work: "The government was attacked from three sides—first the ground-level mobilisation done by Uday's team, then the technical side where we brought out three volumes of technical books on the subject, and third the legal side using the courts. We learnt from the Narmada Bachao Andolan experience, where Medha Patkar approached the courts directly and they shot it down, and decided that PMANE would not do the same. The people's movement would be the people's movement and the legal issues would be handled by us."

Reinforcing the commonly held belief that this is a fight between unequals, fellow PMANE leader Pushparyan also points out that they are a small group agitating against a mammoth government. "They are powerful, we are powerless. We only have some knowledge and information about the plant which we are able to mobilise," he says. "Moreover, since the movement is predominantly by Catholic fishermen and women, for the ordinary citizens out on the streets of Tamil Nadu, it is branded a Christian movement or a fishermen's movement. So we are a small community without much support from other communities, and that makes it a David versus Goliath fight," says Ryan (as he prefers to be called). "But we continue to file a lot of RTIs (right to information petitions), collect information through our expert team and legal team. So it is not just nuisance value. We are very active in formulating our charges (against the plant), and whatever we said with respect to sub-standard parts and other things has proved true," he claims.

The burly, bespectacled priest-turned-activist had worked with the fishing community for 19 years and was familiar with the issues involved when he was called by Idinthakarai's parish priest on August 10, 2011, to help calm agitated villagers. Their distress was occasioned by the NPCIL advisory in *Dinakaran* on action to be taken in case of an accident at KKNPP.

Those living closest to the plant—the people of Koodan-kulam and Idinthakarai—demanded to know why NPCIL had not issued notices to their villages instead of in neighbouring Kanyakumari, says Ryan. The villagers were already in a combative mood after the hot runs with dummy fuel loaded in the reactor. "I live 80 km away in Tirunelveli. I came and addressed the people who were gathered here; I told them that even though the plant was going to be inaugurated soon, we could still fight if we were united. Koodankulam villagers were very eager to join. I warned them that if they joined they would need to be united throughout and face many trials; they could be arrested, they could die...I told them that there were a lot of issues we could fight on but for each we would need time and unity. That's how I motivated them. They were convinced, and we formed a 70-member committee from the 120 people gathered there, divided them into two groups and sent them to neighbouring villages along the coast of Kanyakumari as well as Tuticorin district. Two days later, Uday Kumar joined in," says Ryan, recalling the genesis of the movement that was to change his life in a myriad ways.

On August 12, 2011, at Idinthakarai, Uday Kumar addressed the assembled people of Koodankulam and Idinthakarai, quickly becoming the coordinator and face of the PMANE struggle committee while Ryan supervised all media interactions and online announcements. The duo—supported by a core team of activists such as Father Mahipa Jesuraj, Muhilan, an expert scientific team and legal and environmental experts—began a journey that has seen remarkable highs and lows. Almost two years later, their destination is still not in sight.

For the protestors however, the journey, the protest

itself, is the destination, beginning with the choice of women as torchbearers of the struggle, and emphasising the completely democratic decision-making procedure, laying the responsibility—and the onus—on all. Village committee meetings are held every week, community leaders from each village are represented including women and youth, and decisions are debated and taken collectively.

"We are very accountable to the people, so they like us. Every day we tell them what is happening on the KKNPP issue, we consult them on each decision, ask for their help, interact with them regularly—that bridges the gap and creates a bond," Ryan explains earnestly.

This transparency and collective decision-making is in stark contrast to NPCIL's style of functioning. The constant refrain one hears in Idinthakarai, Koodankulam, Vijaypathi, Perumenal and Vairavikinaru is that no one came and talked to them about the nuclear plant, the trial runs, the mock drill or disaster management procedure, the environment impact assessment or EIA report. No one organised a public hearing, which is mandatory. Villagers living less than 2 km from the nuclear plant lament that nobody from the government or NPCIL visited them to allay their fears about radiation in case of an accident, or reassure them about the safety measures taken for storage of radioactive material, or the effects of hot water discharge from the plant into the sea and its impact on marine life.

Uday outlines the PMANE stand: "This is a project affecting the people, so they must have the final say, not the court or any other body. If the people decide not to have the plant, then don't; if the project-affected people say, "yes, we can live with it" then they should be allowed to decide. That is why the EIA and public hearing are conducted. So that the local people can decide. We told the central government and state government expert team that we are not the masters of these people, we only see ourselves as their servants and representatives. So meet the people in the nearby villages and if you convince them and they agree with you and allow you to go ahead, then do so. But nobody came."

From the first resolution passed on Independence Day, 2011, by the gram sabhas or village councils of Koodankulam, Vijaypathi, Koothankuzhi and Levinjipuram demanding an immediate shutdown of the Koodankulam plant, to the first one-day relay hunger strike the following day, August 16, at Idinthakarai, to the 678th day of protest by the women of Idinthakarai, the movement against KKNPP has used (and sometimes invented) different strategies of dissent.

They have held daily relay protests at Idinthakarai in the Gandhian tradition of non-violent *satyagraha*; they have picketed and burnt effigies of the plant on the roads; they have launched motorbike rallies and candlelight processions, children's rallies and boat rallies; they have buried themselves in the sand up to their necks in sea sieges; tonsured their heads and formed human chains; even walked into the sea in *jalsatyagrahas*, braving the wrath of the state.

In almost two years of continuous and sustained opposition to KKNPP, beginning August 2011, the agitation has faced a severe backlash from the state. People speak resentfully of *lathi*-charges, of arrests at all hours on charges of sedition and waging war against the state for attending a protest rally against the plant, of their young sons being denied visas to work abroad because their passports are held back on 'trumped-up' charges, of police threats and taunts, of artificially created power cuts that last days, of income tax raids, and of the ubiquitous 'foreign funding' charge. It is a litany of what one must expect if one takes on a prestigious state project and dares to question its safety, need and viability.

Uday and Ryan are resigned to queries about this being a 'sponsored' agitation; it is obviously a question they have had to answer many times. "Just yesterday I got a comment on Facebook that I have got money from the US. I will probably have to live with this stigma for the rest of my life, but it doesn't bother me as long as I am clean and my conscience is clear. You cannot convince everyone in the world. The other weapon they use against men in public life is womanising and that came up recently although they did not use my name. They used someone else's name. How can you prove that you are clean? We don't take it seriously. But this huge state of India hasn't produced even one shred of evidence for any of this. That itself proves that we are not getting any money from any foreign country, and we have been speaking against the American (nuclear) plants not only after John Kerry's visit but before also. We said we are sons of the soil and we don't want India to have nuclear power from any country," declares Uday firmly.

Ryan explains how the movement is funded: "It is purely people's money. It works because they contribute each week. Outsiders who come for the protests contribute; some who live in coastal villages and work in foreign countries also contribute (to the cause). Some give Rs 50,000 or Rs 100,000; they also give as a village, not just as individuals. Women give 1/10th of their salary each week in this village and a few other villages also. In many places, fishermen give 1/10th of their catch every week. That is enough. But that perception of the movement being foreign-funded still exists in spite of the government conducting raids and searching our homes. They were not able to find anything. It's a false campaign."

Uday elaborates that the village committee handles the finances as PMANE does not have a bank account. His own bank accounts and those of his wife Meera were scrutinised by the CBI and CID but no charges of impropriety were ever proved, claims Uday.

After the launch of the relay fasts/protests in August 2011, the first phase of the agitation continued with indefinite hunger strikes through the first half of September till the leaders met Chief Minister J Jayalalitha on September 21, 2011 and the Tamil Nadu cabinet passed a resolution to halt work at Koodankulam 'till the people's fears were allayed'—the last being a popular phrase used in the context of PAP.

A few days later, on October 7, 2011 PMANE leaders met with Prime Minister Manmohan Singh in New Delhi. Isn't it rare for leaders of people's movements to get the chance to have a dialogue with chief ministers and the prime minister, I ask Uday Kumar curiously. And did it help at all?

Uday describes the meetings in detail: "We met the chief minister first to convince her to pass a resolution in cabinet (to halt work at the plant) which was a huge success. Then we met Prime Minister Dr Manmohan Singh. I spoke for 20 minutes. He listened to me patiently and carefully but I could tell he was very angry because he did not like a group of people questioning his nuclear policy and his project. He was visibly angry and impatient but controlling himself; I could tell by his body language. The minister of state in the PMO, V Narayansamy, national security advisor Shivshankar Menon, NPCIL chief S K Jain were also there. The fact that they let me speak and listened to me was a big thing and I gave the memorandum, underlining some points. At the end, the PM shook hands with me saying they would stop work at the plant but continue with the maintenance work. But I said: 'Please stop that work also as there is no way to distinguish between the two.' He agreed to look into it. We brought all of them together and made them agree to the proposition that all work had to be stopped. They were proceeding with the commissioning of the project and working on that when we met the PM and asked him to halt all work, conduct a thorough investigation and then decide whether or not to go ahead."

The triumph of the meeting was shortlived. The PM's *volte face* in the form of a letter to Chief Minister Jayalalitha in favour of continuing work at the plant resulted in exactly that. As work continued undeterred at the plant, PMANE protestors started the second and third phase of their hunger strikes along with road blockades and massive sieges around the reactor site. A black flag protest, mid-sea protest, motorbike rally, Tsunami Day children's rally, Koodankulam Chalo march—in the months following, the PMANE struggle committee was determined in its efforts to keep the momentum going and the issue alive in public memory.

But the real test and challenge was to come later, after the Sankarankoil assembly constituency election on March 19, 2012, when it was Chief Minister Jayalalitha's turn to do a *volte face* and pass a cabinet resolution in the Tamil Nadu assembly in favour of KKNPP. The very next day even as over 4,000 villagers gathered at Idinthakarai—some from neighbouring coastal villages—to protest the decision to start operations at the plant, security forces were deployed in and around Koodankulam/Idinthakarai; 199 people were arrested across the state, Section 144 was imposed, and access to Idinthakarai by road was blocked by 6,000 armed policemen, leading to an acute shortage of essential commodities including food supplies (even milk), water, fuel, oil and diesel. People from neighbouring villages brought in supplies for the beleaguered villagers of Idinthakarai on boats, using the limited coastal access.

A fact-finding team comprising senior journalist Sam Rajappa, senior lecturer Dr Gladston Xavier, Madurai bench high court advocate Porkodi Karnan and PUCL members N MahadevanThambi and P Rajan visiting the protest site a few days later (March 30-31, 2012) reported that "the frequency and manner in which the police have filed cases against peaceful protestors clearly exposes that the police's intent never was to uphold the rule of law, but to crush any dissenting voices". The report stated that even in the previous year, the police had filed 107 FIRs against 55,795 people and 'others' between September-December 2011; of these, 6,800 people were charged with sedition and/or 'waging war against the state'. In a press interview (Firstpost, April 2012) Vijayendra Bidari, superintendent of police, Tirunelveli district, rejected the figures quoted by the fact-finding team, denying harassment and explaining that "in multiple cases the accused are the same, hence the figure adds up". The fact-finding report on the suppression of democratic dissent in anti-nuclear protests by the Tamil Nadu government found PMANE to be a "genuine people's movement" using non-violent and democratic means for its struggle.

After an eventful nine-day hunger strike in March 2012, Uday, Ryan, Muhilan, Father Jesuraj and other PMANE activists resumed a life that would never be normal again. They would not be able to move out of Idinthakarai for fear of arrest since they had all been charged with sedition and waging war against the state.

Their future, their family life, their goals were now inextricably linked with the future of the struggle against KKNPP, irrespective of how long and uncertain the outcome was or how difficult the journey.

I ask the leaders about their voluntary exile and why this particular village is a safe haven. Ryan replies with a smile: "This is one of the biggest fishing villages where the people are vigorous and valiant and the police fears them. When people are divided the police takes advantage, when there is unity among people then nobody can come in. As soon as the police enter Idinthakarai, someone rings the church bell and everyone assembles here, ready to face any situation. The police then back off. "

At the time of our March 2012 hunger strike and police harassment, recalls Uday, thousands of people slept around the parish priest's house at night to protect them from a midnight arrest while several young men guarded them round the clock.

The parish priest's residence provides spartan sanctuary to the PMANE leaders; an alcove-like room adjacent to the small office has one steel bed with a straw *chattai* (mat) draped over it. Another *charpoy* (wooden bed) stands propped up against the wall. There is only one bathroom in this house shared by the priests and PMANE leaders. Two flowery curtains give a modicum of privacy to the miniscule space that Uday Kumar sleeps in late every night; the space under the bed and the table next to it is crammed untidily with old newspapers and large bags. All the clothes pegs on the wall opposite the beds are noticeably occupied.

Next to this makeshift 'bedroom' are two rooms where the priests carry out their routine parish work; the dining room opens out into a spacious backyard which is the preferred meeting place for impromptu discussions and interviews.

This limited domain—in addition of course to the homes of the supporting villagers—has been thrust upon the PMANE leaders because of legal cases filed against them and a total of 227,000 people opposing KKNPP. Under normal circumstances, the nuts and bolts of running a movement, organisational details and minutiae of paperwork is assigned to young volunteer teams in rotation; in this case Uday, Ryan and Muhilan take on a substantial share, with expert teams providing back-up support.

Sitting under the banyan tree in the backyard on one of the many plastic chairs hospitably kept there for visitors, 45-year-old Muhilan—the aggressive, sloganeering frontrunner at major PMANE events—reels off statistics related to the legal cases; this is what he has been tracking for the last two years, all of the court cases against the villagers and PMANE activists, their bail work, documents and other information related to jails and the police.

On his way to attend his son's birthday in his native place Erode, the agricultural activist with a mechanical engineering degree was one of the first to be arrested in March 2012. Muhilan spent three months in jail on charges of sedition. "There are more than 100 cases of sedition, waging war against the state, attempt to murder and damage to public property," he says, providing details, 18,143 people booked under 'attempt to murder', 15,565 under 'public property damage', 13,850 under 'waging war against the state' and 21 cases of 'sedition' against 8,956 people.

The total number, he declares, is 380 cases against 227,000 people. The explanation for this staggering figure is simple: the cases are filed against Uday Kumar and 5,000 accused, Pushparayan and 3,000 accused... In this way, explains Muhilan, the total number of accused is much higher than the actual 15,000 who were present at the agitation on March 19, 2012, and the 199 people who were arrested included 134 men, 42 women, 22 youth and one mentally challenged person.

A queue of at least 20-30 people would come to meet him every day in connection with jailed relatives, says Muhilan; today that number has considerably reduced.

Ryan joins us for a mid-morning tea break, giving me the only copy of an English newspaper that is delivered to their residence every day. He elaborates on the restricted mobility that is now taken for granted by all of them. "After March 12, 2012, we have not stepped out of this village; we go to neighbouring villages only on side roads. We are safe here. If we go out of the village we might be arrested and that would wreck the movement, so we cannot take any risks. Like Uday I also have cases against me—sedition, waging war, everything. I am 'Accused Number 2'," he says laconically.

Isn't living in exile, away from family and friends, with no clear indication of the journey's end a hard price to pay for leading the movement, I ask Ryan. And isn't his family—his wife, son and father—paying the price too? He nods agreement instantly but goes on to add that it is a "worthy sacrifice for a greater cause". "My son is still young and waits for me every day, expecting me to come home. He needs my support," says Ryan.

When do you think you will be able to go home?

"It depends on the people. Whenever we have a formal kind of closure, if the government listens to the people or if we are able to force the government to listen," he shrugs.

Muhilan's family visits him once in three months. "To get something you have to lose something," he says matter-of-factly. "My parents are uneducated but I have learnt from people and society, because someone fought for our rights. So I feel I should also give back to people," he tells me earnestly.

By this time, Father 'Mahipa' Jesuraj, Father Jayakumar, a few novice priests and Uday have all gathered around the tree and are discussing the day's news and events over their customary 'red' tea. Muhilan engages in friendly banter with the efficient lady cook-housekeeper who keeps an open kitchen for all residents and visitors to the house. Fish curry and rice are staples, given their proximity to the sea, but other South Indian fare like *idlis, dosas, puttu* are regulars too.

The courtyard, which is surrounded by leafy green trees, has a straw roof, a water tank and a large dustbin nearby. Everyone washes their own plates after meals. The area is clearly an impromptu gathering place. Two benches and several plastic chairs are placed invitingly for people to chat, eat, read newspapers, work on legal files (like Muhilan), conduct catechism for children preparing for their first Communion with the novice priests, or simply to observe (like me).

Ryan and Uday go into a huddle over the imminent visit of a political functionary—at least two or three visitors seek a brief audience with the PMANE leaders every day. Ryan instructs the ever-helpful Amal Raj Leon, unofficial translator for all visitors as he is the only multilingual person in the village speaking Malayalam, Hindi and English in addition to Tamil. Two anti-nuke activists from Australia are expected later in the day, radio professionals visiting Idinthakarai for much the same reasons I am, to gather and tell stories.

Father Jayakumar counsels the novice priests in another corner, unfazed that his backyard and indeed his home have been taken over by the PMANE movement and turned into a temporary headquarters. I drink my tea silently, letting the conversation swirl around me—I don't really have a choice as it is all in Tamil, interspersed with frequent guffaws and teasing. A strong sense of camaraderie coupled with robust enthusiasm are easily discernible among the leaders of the struggle committee; their 682-day exile (so far!) must have its share of lonely angst but for the most part it remains hidden under a patina of 'satisfaction in fulfilling people's needs'.

Uday gets emotional as he says: "I feel all these villagers have gathered around the struggle mainly because of us—we said we would lead them and be with them. It is impossible to desert them now, no matter what the consequences are, even if it is death. I am 53 now and I have seen everything in life. If you cheat these people, let them stand in the middle of the stream and run away, it would be a shameful thing because this is a principle we have embarked on. We should stick to it. And we will succeed."

Today Uday's life has come full circle. A Nagercoil native, after finishing his graduate and post-graduate studies in Madurai and Kerala universities he left his hometown to teach English in Ethiopia for six years, moving to the US to complete another Masters degree in peace studies from Notre Dame and a PhD in political science from the University of Hawaii. After a 12-year stint in the US, working as co-director of programmes at the Institute on Race and Poverty at the University of Minnesota, Minneapolis, for three years and teaching conflict-resolution and peace studies at various American universities while his wife Meera—a story of 'marry at first sight'—worked at an adoption agency, the couple returned to India in January 2001 with their two young sons, to run a school together in Nagercoil (they had earlier purchased 15 acres of land near the town and founded

SACCER—South Asian Community Centre for Education and Research, a trust for educational initiatives such as their school).

Sitting in his tiny office, away from that "safe and wonderful" life of teaching schoolchildren in Nagercoil, Uday reveals a small part of his innermost feelings. "Even as a student I have had this streak for organising people, taking the initiative and working for a public cause. So I am happy that I am contributing something small to the community, that my education and talent is being used for nameless, faceless, powerless people. On the other hand, I am getting a little scared now that maybe I'm part of a current whose speed and flow I cannot control; the uncertainty and anxiety involved and the huge burden it puts on you has scared me a little bit. I am also a little concerned about my family because it has been almost two years now. Meera and the boys (Surya and Satya) are taking the brunt of all this; they are paying a huge price," he admits regretfully.

He describes the "very pleasant and beautiful life" they led in Nagercoil after their conscious decision to come back and bring up their children in India so that they would grow up with the rest of the family. "My flexible schedules would allow me to teach in universities in the US and Europe, bringing in quick bucks, a few thousand euros which is a lot of money in India. Then I would come back to Nagercoil and teach social science at our school and also look after the administration," says Uday with a smile. "Of course I kept working on the anti-nuclear issue and went for conferences around the world. I was passionate about it but I never thought in my wildest dreams that I would find myself leading a major movement like this."

I ask him how he deals with the contrast in his life today where he is a virtual prisoner in Idinthakarai, with little privacy and a fair amount of privations compared to the idyllic times of three years ago. He credits his wife Meera for her supportive role despite it being very hard on her and the children. "My younger son thinks it is like a government job and asked me: 'Why don't you take two months leave and come home?' The older one, who is 15, understands that this is a struggle, that we are doing it for the people, and luckily our children share our political values. My older son does not want to buy rich-looking clothes, he says he wants to be one with the local people," says Uday with visible pride.

~

Nagercoil isn't too far from Idinthakarai, just 40-odd km, approximately an hour's car journey on pot-holed roads. I choose to take the Tamil Nadu State Transport bus instead, instantly exchanging speed and comfort for local flavour and a lively experience. Since the bus arrives almost two hours late at the adjoining village bus stop (there is no state transport bus directly to Idinthakarai), it is packed to capacity with passengers, mostly old ladies and younger women carrying enormous bags and parcels. Men and women are neatly divided into separate sections and the rule is strictly adhered to; since there is no vacant seat I spend the next 45 minutes hopping from one foot to another, clutching the handrest, communicating with signs and smiles with the old *pattis* (Tamil for grandmothers) who attempt to ask me inquisitive questions about where I have come from.

After many shuddering halts at designated stops and passing through scenic village montages, the bus makes its way two hours later into the noisy, bustling small town of Nagercoil. In a short while, I am sitting in Meera Uday Kumar's neat drawing room waiting for her to finish her telephone call.

The family home is modest and unassuming; an ordinary, middle class Tamilian house, the living room furnished simply with a wooden sofa, a few chairs including some bright blue plastic ones, a TV set on a trolley with bundles of newspapers underneath, and the ever-popular calendars of gods and goddesses on the walls. The single bars of the wooden window grills reveal a resplendent green courtyard with trees, sunshine and lots of space for children to play in.

Parking his bike outside the entrance door, 15-year-old Surya, eldest son of Meera and Uday Kumar, walks in, shyly acknowledging my introduction. By his own admission—and to his mother's regret—he has matured a lot faster than his age warrants, courtesy his father's continued absence from home. Tall, slim and good-looking, Surya admits that he feels responsible as the 'man of the house' today; he is proud of his father and wants to follow in his footsteps by doing things for others, not just for his family, when he grows up. "I don't want to lead people but I want to save the earth, conserve forests and protect animals. We used to watch programmes on Animal Planet; now I also watch cricket," he informs me solemnly. Both boys are animal rights activists, says their mother, "they keep chickens in the yard".

What are the things you did with your father or as a family that you miss most now, I ask Surya. "We don't do anything as a family, we only eat as a family," is his surprisingly blunt answer.

What would you like to do, I prod.

"We both like to play and they both like to work. What can we say/like about their work," he asks in return. An embarrassed Meera hurriedly adds that they miss out on a lot due to Uday's long absence. Surya interjects nonchalantly: "We miss him but our normal life is not so affected. Even when he is here I go to school and do my homework."

Our workaholic schedules are responsible for this, admits Meera wryly. Satya, the youngest member of the family nods agreement but refuses to talk to me; he vanishes into another room to watch TV with his grandmother.

Visits to Idinthakarai to meet their father vary according to the children's schedules, sometimes once a fortnight or once a month; summer vacations mean a lot more time. The one rule Meera religiously follows is that each family member talks to Uday every day, updating him, sharing the details of their lives with each other.

Meera Uday Kumar is "living her dream", even if that means single-handedly running a school, overseeing property issues, social causes, her children's work and taking care of her elderly parents and in-laws who live with her.

Disarmingly frank and emotive, the diminutive Meera, dressed formally in a crisp cotton sari, a red *bindi* on her forehead, talks of the life skills she has learned in the years coping alone, away from her husband. "People look at you differently. Not everyone gets the opportunity to look at things with equanimity. I have learnt to take criticism, to ignore, to avoid people and to walk away. I don't watch TV when there are discouraging remarks being made about Uday. If you lend your ears to negativity it will get to you, and I know the things they (some people) say are not true; it is like distancing yourself from hearsay. I try to spend time within myself and sort things out because those fears have to be dealt with," she reasons.

She tells me about her college years—completing a women's studies course and then an MA in English literature, and then teaching in a school; about meeting Uday for the first time on a street in Chennai and both of them deciding in five minutes that they wanted to marry each other; about living a life of "shared responsibility" in the US for 12 years; and eventually about coming home to jointly start a school, which was always her dream.

Did she ever resent his total involvement in the Koodankulam issue that has forced her to power her dream on her own? Her reply is generous, with not a trace of self-pity. "We were in sync so I knew it was his only passion as he was always talking about it. If you really love a person how can you hold him back and not let him do what he wants? If I had held him back he would never have been happy, and if he was not happy then how could I have been? I don't think there was anything large-hearted about it at all," she says honestly.

She also believes—and so does Uday—that there is a larger force, some goodwill, or Nature or the Universe that is taking care of him. "That goodwill is giving him immunity against the many people who may not like what he says. I cannot protect or hide him away. If I stay positive then that will help him. So we always tell him we are fine and taking care of ourselves. He does the same. We don't want to frighten or burden each other; it is a conscious thing we do now—I go there only when I am alright. When I go there he needs to charge me and I need to charge him. Yesterday I had a bad day and asked him if he wanted to hear about it. And he said he didn't. So it does get awfully lonely for both of us..." her voice trails off momentarily, traces of vulnerability obvious in the extremely telling remark.

What do you consider to be your husband's biggest victory in terms of the struggle he is leading, I ask her.

She perks up and answers immediately: "People have got leadership training; they have learnt to discuss all kinds of issues, not just the Koodankulam plant's closure! In the last three years so many people have visited this little village (Idinthakarai), so youngsters have been fed with a lot of critical thinking and courage, the knowledge that you don't have to be ordinary. If you think there is something wrong then you should say it; and if you say it through the right means you can get the point across to the other person. Don't hide because the other party is intimidating you; persevere and stand your ground. This is the positive message the movement has given to the next generation. I want my sons to grow up in the company of such people; their prime should be a breeze, not beset with many problems," she ends with a smile.

As dusk settles and the evening lamp is lit in the puja room, Ponmoni Amma, Uday's 77-year-old mother, joins in the conversation, Meera playing translator.

"Many people I interviewed told me that they see Uday Kumar as god. How do you feel being the mother of such a person," I ask. Meera laughs as Amma beams with pride. "I feel very proud that he is bringing about such change, helping everyone. I hope he becomes even more famous. I taught him to help others, be honest, spread love and not get swayed by money. I hope he emerges victorious. They should shut the plant and whatever he wants should happen," she says simply.

Her only wish is to hug her son tight when he comes home, she adds lovingly. "That would be the biggest joy for me—I would not have experienced such joy in the past, nor will I experience it again in future!"

It's with those passionate words echoing in my head that I make my way back to Idinthakarai in the dark—by car this time. I wonder when that particular wish, along with the wishes of the protesting villagers, will be fulfilled.

~

The early morning Mass at Idinthakarai's majestic church sees several devout worshippers, but there is a much larger contingent of inadvertent listeners too courtesy the loudspeakers artfully arranged at key places in the village, relaying the service at 5.30 am and then again at 6.30 pm.

Some 300 devotees throng the evening Mass as I try to make my way to the red-and-gold altar at the stately Lourdes church, past row upon row of men and women with scarves covering their heads, past little children seated in the front rows, till I am able to see Father 'Mahipa' Jesuraj in the pulpit, dressed in red-and-gold robes, about to begin his sermon.

There is near-total silence for the next hour as he holds forth; I catch the words 'Koodankulam' a few times and the Tamil words for 'people's struggle'—*makal porattam*—that I have managed to learn so far. After the sermon, as the church bells ring, he holds aloft the sign of the cross on all four sides and leaves. The formally dressed choir boys and girls sing their hymns to the accompaniment of a keyboard player, while a choir girl takes joss sticks and twirls them around the church. As hymns resound from the loudspeakers outside and through the village, those kneeling outside the church—in the marble foyer and even on the sands of the *pandal*—continue their worshipful stance.

People here are god-fearing, but what exactly is the role of the Catholic Church in this movement, I ask Father 'Mahipa' Jesuraj the next morning after breakfast, in the same courtyard which is relatively quiet at this time. Officially the church doesn't take part in the movement, he informs me solemnly; individuals do. "My own bishop in Tirunelveli told me right in the beginning that he faced political and government pressure and that I should go back. I told him: 'I think I am ordained for this issue.' He then said he would not be able to stand by me in case of any problems. I answered that if I am working for the people they would stand by me; otherwise god would take care of me, the bishop need not worry." Father Jesuraj chuckles reminiscently.

"I have a double role: I am a leader in the PMANE struggle committee and I am a priest. That helps a lot because the people here are god-fearing and obey the word of a priest. What leaders say onstage we say from the pulpit in church—we give the same idea, speak in the same tone, that is why the people easily understood and committed themselves to the issue," he says frankly.

I ask him if mixing religion and politics in this way, propagating activism during Mass was acceptable. His reply is both succinct and apposite. "You have to say the word of god according to the situation. According to the context you have to explain the text—without context there is no text!" He laughs at the bemused expression on my face. The answer is so simple and yet so layered. I ask him for an example from the Bible that reflects the current situation with the struggle and he immediately quotes Jesus standing up for the truth.

Like other PMANE leaders, Father Jesuraj too has not left Idinthakarai since October 2012; he is also named in the 380 cases filed against the leaders and describes being surrounded by the police when he went to his village for a feast. Luckily, he says, he managed to escape.

He mentions other forms of harassment—"Uday, Ryan and my names, telephone numbers and addresses were published in the *Dinamalar* newspaper, saying that we were leading the anti-

Koodankulam agitation and were responsible for the power shortage in the state, and that people should talk directly to us. People would call us all the time, even at 2 and 3 at night and condemn us in foul language. They would threaten to kill us and our families, saying: 'Because of you we have no power.' We had to turn off our phones."

Switching back to the present and to the future, I ask him where he sees the movement headed, given that everyone in the village says their strength and morale emanates from god. It's akin to spiritual power versus nuclear power, isn't it, I say to him, and he nods agreement.

The parish priest, Father Jayakumar, plays an important role, he says. That's one reason why spiritual power gives them strength. We all sit together, everyone plays their part, our teamwork is good and we take decisions collectively. But the people have to decide ultimately, he ends.

≈

The afternoon sun glints through pinprick openings in the *pandal's* roof, casting intricate patterns on the sand below as the women sit listening in rapt attention to Uday Kumar sharing stories of another indomitable lady of another era—Rosa Parks and her struggle to get both black and white Americans equal rights to sit in buses. Today there are 25 women sitting in protest. Some, like Xavier, listen carefully; some sit on the outskirts of the semi-circle around Uday, Ryan, Muhilan and Father Jesuraj, continuing their *beedi*-making and tending to their children. As the story reaches its triumphant end, everyone listens attentively, happy in Rosa's victory. Ryan ends the briefing by passing around a schedule of activities that includes the travel plans of women who will carry the protest message beyond Idinthakarai.

I trail Uday back to his office to ask a few follow-up questions before he begins work on his computer, answering mails, collecting and collating information and a myriad other tasks related to the movement.

Why use the Rosa Parks analogy here, I ask."People like to listen to stories like this. The reason I mentioned Rosa Parks is to share that revolutions happen all of a sudden from totally unexpected sources. It is not one party in the vanguard that carries out revolutions. When speakers come here they talk about other stories, give examples. People here like that. We talk about things they can identify with; we invoke the Bhopal gas tragedy and the way Rajiv Gandhi and Arjun Singh helped Warren Anderson (Union Carbide chief) escape, and how people are still running from pillar to post (for justice)," explains Uday.

On a different note I ask him how he reacts to adulation from the women, to statements such as "for us Uday Kumar is like god".

He brushes it aside instantly: "I don't take it seriously. When people talk to me like that I divert the conversation or cut them off sometimes. It's a huge responsibility and already it's a huge burden. People tend to dump everything on you—their expectations, dreams and desires. It's a kind of outpouring of all their emotions. I have to invent a way of keeping myself isolated from all that. I listen to them and tell them I have the same kind of frustrations and problems as they do."

Is morale flagging? Is it fair to expect the women to sit in protest day after day with no visible response from the authorities?

"It's very unfair and in any other community this wouldn't have been possible. For these fishermen, daily life is a struggle. They go out to sea and fight the waves. Struggle is their bottom line; their very existence. That is the reason they are able to withstand all this pressure and keep fighting. Morale gets low at times, especially when powerful forces come and divide the community, offering bribes, intimidating us and using all kinds of dirty tricks. Despite all that, we have managed to sustain this struggle for almost 678 days, which is a big achievement," Uday answers.

Do you ever get the feeling that you're disconnected from the rest of the world, cooped up here in this village?

I always like to consider the cup half-full rather than half-empty, says Uday with a smile. "Given the fact that we've not left Idinthakarai in the last one-and-a-half years, to still make news is astounding. We made the headlines on (Tamil) television channels three days ago during the John Kerry protest. Yesterday, all the Tamil Nadu papers carried news about our issue; of course the rest of India or the world may not know much, but even so a friend of mine from Minnesota told me that a Minnesota public radio channel and newspaper talked about this issue. Another friend saw a news report on our struggle on BBC News in Hong Kong. So it is there and not there. People in Delhi and the rest of the country do talk about it; it is not a completely dismal picture," he explains.

"Besides, Amnesty International friends helped us a lot. They put out an SOS call whenever we got arrested, harassed or tortured. They wrote letters from Canada, the US, Australia, Germany, Austria, France, Spain, to the prime minister and the chief minister; they sent us copies of the letters. The PMO knows that these guys are well-connected. The German and French media came, interviewed us and published stories. It's not like we are totally isolated," declares Uday with a flourish.

Ryan, who sends out press releases on a regular basis, says however that while the local media response is quick and substantial, mainstream media only covers 'prominent' events like sieges at the plant, that too for a limited duration. Most television channels get their footage from local stringers instead of travelling to the villages for detailed reporting. "We wrote a letter to all the media houses asking them to look into the KKNPP issue, saying 'you are the fourth pillar of democracy', but we got no response," says Ryan.

Nupur Basu, who analysed media coverage of the Koodankulam agitation in the online media watchdog, *The Hoot*, corroborates much of Ryan's plaint. She quotes Sadanand Menon, senior Chennai-based journalist and art critic in her article:

> The Koodankulam 'coverage' has been distinguished by apathy and half-heartedness in the English and Tamil press. One realises the shallowness in our media when it comes to such issues. There's not even a passing expertise or familiarity with the subject, with the result that the official line is what they get impressed by. The big English dailies have made do with reports from local correspondents without sending more informed editors out there and creating much-needed interface and debate. Nevertheless, *The Hindu* editorials have been good.

The Indian Express and *Tehelka* magazine provided consistent ground zero reports on the people's agitation, especially during the tumultuous September 2012 period. English television news channels covered the Koodankulam issue sporadically—ground reports during the September 2012 police-protestors face-off telecast on NDTV, CNN-IBN and Times Now, among others—

while the occasional debate or talk show highlighted polarised views. Tamil channels like Sun TV and Jaya TV were strongly partisan in favour of KKNPP. Social networks such as Facebook and Twitter as well as citizen journalists reporting about Koodankulam became an alternative source of information about the movement.

What would you like to do to get more people to become aware of your struggle, I ask Uday. His answer is illuminating and analytical: "The English and Hindi television channels do give time but very sporadically and superficially so a deeper debate about the intricate issues would be good. And some newspaper articles and columns would be good. But then in a country where 60-70% of the people may not watch or read the news none of this is any substitute; on the other hand, this 60-70% readily identify themselves with us. They live in harmony with nature and it is their story. They don't hurt people or nature. It is the middle class and political class who are doing more damage, and they will never be converted to our side. No matter what you say, they won't accept it. And they own the media and have everything. For us it is impossible right now to go the length and breadth of the nation to spread the message," says Uday realistically.

To a limited extent, the women of Idinthakarai, members of the protest movement, *do* travel as ambassadors delivering their unique message of struggle and survival at the invitation of anti-nuclear forums such as the Coalition for Nuclear Disarmament and Peace (CNDP) or to the sites of other nuclear plants like Haripur in West Bengal. They share their experiences of how the state has treated them, solicit support, mark Hiroshima Day, keeping the spirit of the agitation alive both outside and inside Idinthakarai.

The leaders ensure motivation levels are high by planning at least two programmes a month. Ryan shares their strategy: "We make it a point to gather as many people as possible onstage so there is participation. We show films and recorded programmes. After we began our protest people have started listening to the news and debates more keenly, so when we show videos they really enjoy them."

For the leaders who have been living at the parish priest's residence for over 18 months now in virtual exile, with brief, intermittent visits from their families, a routine day could begin as early as 8.30 am, if there is an event or protest march scheduled, and end at 2.30 am after the online communications and social media interactions have been completed. Ryan and Uday use blogs, Twitter and Facebook to share news, opinions and campaigns not just about the Koodankulam plant but also about nuclear energy, alternative energy and global movements on nuclear power.

This is a movement that liberally uses digital technologies to empower and mobilise people and people's opinions.

Late (and solitary) breakfasts are the norm in the house while lunch is a more collective affair with visitors trooping in at all times to meet the PMANE leaders or the priests—the official residents!

Afternoons are spent interacting with more visitors or villagers and holding the daily briefing for the women sitting in protest. Village committee meetings that take place at different venues can go on for extended periods depending on the issue being discussed; they are also held regularly and/or on request, depending on need.

≈

Every evening, an hour before the loudspeakers begin relaying the customary hymns, Father Jesuraj takes a brisk and barefoot walk along the narrow, sandy path on the seashore. I decide to follow his healthy example and soon find a rag-tag team of small children following me, imitating my walk with amused giggles. Half-an-hour later as I make my way to Uday's office, I find him and Ryan hunched over their computers working energetically on a press release that has to go out the next day. The tiny room is plunged into darkness five minutes later as a result of a power cut. In the time it takes for the small generator to power up, Uday and Ryan regale me with stories of living without electricity—and other essentials—for days on end during the infamous September 2012 clampdown on Idinthakarai. I ask them to save that story for another day.

Chapter Four

"A JAIL WITHIN, A JAIL WITHOUT"
OR THE SEPTEMBER 2012 SIEGE

SOS from children, September 10, 2012, 12 noon
Since this morning we have been sitting in this open parched landscape thinking about our future and lives. We had something to eat and drink, but our minds have been restless. But now we are surrounded by police. They are coming closer and closer. Some are swaying their lathis and also intimidating us.

We are scared that they will not allow us to remain peacefully here.

What is unlawful about sitting in a land that is ours near the sea which has fed us for years?

The only thing we ask for is to live in freedom. We want to grow up strong and healthy. They are using teargas. As I look out, I see my people caught between the sea and police force.

Do please intervene and spread the message of peace. Please do not do this to us; call us or come to us and talk; listen to what we have to say. We want to live in this land and near the sea.

—Children of Idinthakarai and other villages affected by KKNPP
(Extract from *No Echoes Koodankulam* by Anita S)

June 2013, 9.30 am

Protest *pandal*, Idinthakarai

Sixty-year-old Amal Raj Leon walks up the few steps of the church foyer and painstakingly writes 'Day 682' in black on the bulletin board. As he carries out this daily task he tells me how and why he started the countdown. "It was only after 70-80 days that we started writing the days on the board. At that time we were beginning various types of demonstrations, so I proposed this plan. People were not taking it seriously but at one stage I insisted we should maintain this record," he says, the pride visible on his thin face.

He is the first person 'outsiders' go to on their arrival in Idinthakarai—as official translator Amal Raj takes visitors around, explains basic issues related to the plant and the protest, provides information in the required language (in addition to Tamil, he speaks Hindi, English and Malayalam) and facilitates interviews with villagers. He is also the unofficial electrician during major events onstage. As a volunteer he does all of this free of cost. Educated up to Class XI, and retired, he spends his days contributing to a cause he believes in. "I am not giving something I don't have; even in the normal course of events if I can help anyone, I do. So when it's such a big cause, naturally as a man of this village it is my duty. In a way I am helping myself," he says earnestly.

I ask him about the responses he gets from the many visitors the movement attracts on an almost daily basis—students, activists, journalists, anti-nuke groups, political groups, filmmakers. "Many students are afraid to ask questions from both sides—they believe Dr Abdul Kalam's version of the

Koodankulam plant since he was in a high, responsible position and also a scientist," laughs Amal Raj. We explain to them, for example, that Dr Kalam wrote an article in *The Hindu* in support of the plant after spending barely two-and-a-half hours there; it is not possible to do a proper survey in that much time. And he would have spent at least 15-30 minutes on snacks, wouldn't he, asks Amal Raj with a twinkle in his eye.

Didn't he meet the people, I ask.

No, says Amal Raj, we were just opposite the plant. "So we tell students all this."

In the telling and re-telling of the story of Koodankulam, Amal Raj has become fluent in the idiom and philosophy of the agitation, effortlessly presenting its case in the face of any and all arguments.

"I have a hundred percent faith in the success of this agitation. The only uncertain thing is we don't know when to end it because the government doesn't know how to end it—they can neither start it nor close it. They are in a trap," he says.

Are you tense about the plant starting operations, I ask him.

"Yes, of course. If it starts we have to leave this place immediately or perhaps later. Each and every family will be scattered. For example, this is my father's house that I live in; it is my ancestral home. If this is gone, it means my forefathers are disconnected from me. That will be the fate of every family. If I go sit in some other place I can't say that is my village; I have to mention this place as my village. So from there, life starts anew and that is dangerous," explains Amal Raj emotionally.

By now, the number of women entering the *pandal* for the

daily protest has increased. They move past the plastic chairs we are sitting on, shuffling sand and sitting down in little groups with their bits and pieces. Their attitude continues to be cheerful. *"Vanakkam!"* I greet them in Tamil and Xavier, the friendliest and most vocal of the lot, answers in English: "Good morning!"

Today the women are going to talk to me about the form and shape they have given the protest in the 680-odd days of the peaceful struggle—from the first black flag hoisting on Independence Day two years ago to the September siege of the plant in 2012 and the face-off between protestors and the state.

After some internal discussion about who will say what, the women begin: the structure of their narrative reads like a film script with a gradual build-up of momentum, a rich cast of characters both heroic and not so heroic, plot points galore, intense conflicts, differing versions of the same incident, and a climax awaiting resolution, happy or otherwise.

The tale begins in flashback mode.

For 39-year-old Milret, participating in the anti-Koodankulam protests is something of a family tradition. She was 15 when her mother took her along for the first protest in Kanyakumari, in 1989. "The police beat us; they even used guns and one man was killed. Many of us were injured. I still have scars of the wounds caused when I fell as we all ran to safety," claims Milret indignantly. Her mother used to sell crabs near the plant site and would watch scientists "take measurements" at the site, she says. "We were told it was being set up to produce 'current' and a job would be provided for one person from each house. Nobody ever mentioned it was an atomic plant and may be dangerous. And we knew nothing about radiation. At the time of the Kanyakumari protest in 1989 there wasn't much media coverage either or television channels to broadcast our story to the world. Only when we saw what happened in Fukushima did we realise what could happen (here) and that our children may also be affected. I attended protest rallies in Kochi, Thiruvananthapuram and Koodankulam even before these tents were put up two-and-a-half years ago," says Milret, gesturing at the *pandal*.

When her daughter turned 15, Milret brought her along to the *pandal* to sit in protest for the cause; she points to the church foyer and tells me they both slept there after getting hurt on September 10, 2012. "I escaped arrest that day only because I ventured into the water since I can swim. The four women ahead of me got arrested," she tells me conspiratorially.

Like many others in Idinthakarai, Milret has not been able to leave the village because of the numerous legal cases filed in 2012—not withdrawn till date—though her daughter has gone off to study in college.

Vivacious and ever-smiling, she dismisses any suggestion of fatigue in sustaining this long-drawn-out battle. "We will protest until we die. Uday Kumar, Ryan and others have left their families to help us with this protest; they don't go anywhere, they don't earn money, they give their lives for the people. When I see such people around me I feel a boost, like drinking Horlicks," she laughs.

Sitting quietly awaiting her turn, the far more sombre Mary presents an interesting contrast to Milret's infectious enthusiasm. She too has been part of the opposition since the Kanyakumari rally of 1989. She tells me about innovative ways used by the protestors to "protect the whole of Tamil Nadu before it is destroyed".

"When we became aware of the dangers we could not even think of letting go; instead, we fought harder. We tried various ways of agitating: for example, we brought our babies, approximately 40 of them below the age of one, to participate with us and fed them only sugar water," says Mary as I wince in response.

She goes on undeterred: "We buried ourselves in sand up to our necks. We marched in protest from Koodankulam to Radhapuram, from Chettikulam to Levinjipuram to register our pain and anger, but still the government does not recognise it," she says hopelessly.

Other forms of protest include lying prostrate on the road with children, candlelight vigils, tonsuring, blood donations, prayers at the cemetery, children's walks, prayer meetings, numerous sieges at the plant—by land and sea—as well as *jal satyagrahas* and occupations of the seashore.

In keeping with the movement's skills in using social media and the internet to spread their message to the world outside Idinthakarai, updates on the movement by 'the women of Idinthakarai' (as told to various writers) are regularly posted online (on *Dianuke* and other anti-KKNPP websites). These proved especially effective at the time of the police-protestors confrontation in September 2012.

After Chief Minister J Jayalalitha's *volte face* in March 2012 and subsequent support by the Tamil Nadu government of KKNPP, following a report and clean chit on safety submitted by the state expert committee, 199 arrests were made and cases filed against PMANE leaders as protestors defied Section 144 and set up camp near the plant.

Even as the movement upped the ante and swung into agitation mode with indefinite hunger strikes, relay fasts in Koothenkazhi, Koottapuli and Perumanal, candlelight processions on Hiroshima Day and a celebration of the first anniversary of the relay fasts on August 16, the Madras High Court pronounced judgment on August 31, 2012 clearing the commissioning of KKNPP Units 1 and 2 and the loading of uranium fuel at the plant.

The Madras High Court's go-ahead was in response to a writ petition filed by G Sundar Rajan on behalf of PMANE challenging AERB's August 10, 2012, clearance of loading of uranium fuel even though only six of the 17 safety recommendations made by the post-Fukushima government taskforce had been complied with.

The court judgment did, however, direct AERB to ensure that all 17 safety recommendations were complied with. The state government was also asked to set up good schools in and around Koodankulam, build a multi-specialty hospital and a port with cold storage facilities. Offshore safety drills involving local people were also mandated.

In a strong and emotive response to the Madras High Court judgment that went against their demands, the protestors—women at the fore—decided to take their protest out of the confines of their homes, village and protest *pandal* and towards the seashore and KKNPP. They had heard that the uranium fuel was going to be loaded on September 9.

On September 8, in a message posted online, the 'women of Idinthakarai' informed the world via Anita S, environmental educator and communicator, author of the book, *No Echoes Koodankulam*, that their village had become an open jail with roads blocked by sandbags and policemen with assault rifles, including companies of the Rapid Action Force. This did not deter them from moving *en masse*—an estimated 8,000-10,000 people, including women, children and the elderly—towards the seashore on September 9, defying existing prohibitory orders (Section 144) to not venture within 7 km of KKNPP.

On September 9, 2012, the women posted another message through Anita S, about 'what a great day it had been for them'.

Excerpts from this online message:

By 11 am it was decided that we move along the seashore along the Tsunami Rehabilitation Colony from where the plant is shockingly close and visible. The walk in the hot sun, stepping on the warm sand and facing the glare from the white waves only enlivened our spirits.

We were empowered by support from many villages from where groups reached us braving the heavy police force and threat of some kind of stoppage. By 12 noon amidst the rising tide we started moving very close to the hated domes of the KKNPP...

The SP (Superintendent of Police) of Tirunelveli came by noon and told us that we should not do this "unlawful" venture by going so near the power plant. But does everyone expect us to spend our whole life so close to it? Why are they warning us of this when actually they are not bothered about the real danger of living so near this lethal radiation with our children?

By late noon, we were all amazed by the huge support that came in— maybe more than 15,000 (people have) gathered. We decided to sit here in this new venue close to the plant. We announced our decision (to do so) until the Honourable Chief Minister gives her "good word" to us, which is to say that KKNPP will be shut down by stopping the imminent uranium fuel loading.

The youth amongst us has started bringing drinking water. There is some simple porridge being cooked. There will soon be a pandal under which we can take shelter and lights along with basic toilet facilities are being looked after.

Our demands are simple and straight. Please consider our most rightful and just demand for security, peace and right to pursue our life the way we want it. To not live near a toxic nuclear power plant which will silently kill generations and spoil the soil and water. To be able to participate in decisions that are taken for our good and welfare. We do not sense anything unlawful or wrong about all this. Do you?

As the dusk darkens, we sit together and talk. We are a bit tired but our resolve is stronger and clearer. We watch our young ones and are so proud of their perseverance and dedication. We laugh at ourselves and the black T-shirts proclaiming 'Shut KKNPP' that many of us wore over the sari. We hold the white of the flags we carried in our hands symbolising the peaceful march.

Today certainly was a great day for us... Please do carry this message of peace to the world.

—Women of Idinthakarai as told to Anita S

The next day, September 10, 2012, is etched indelibly in the minds and memories of every villager in these parts; either as a result of first-hand experience or because it affected a loved one or friend or acquaintance. Everyone has a story to tell.

Mary relates the events of September 2012 in measured tones though her eyes turn misty at times: "After it was announced on September 8 that uranium fuel would be filled in the plant, there were protests all through the day and night on September 9; at the time the police (who were stationed in the area) were friendly towards us. They even ate our food. But the very next day, on September 10, when we were protesting in a peaceful manner on the seashore about half-a-kilometre from the plant, police personnel beat us, shot at us and even used outdated tear gas on us. We ran for our lives. Many of us got hurt. They really harassed us. I also got very badly hurt. I got boils on my lips but felt better after applying ointment. My eyesight too got blurred," she says.

"Immaculate and I were sitting in the front during the protests," says Mary, "when suddenly the smoke from the tear gas was everywhere and fast increasing. We had no option but to jump into the water, without even knowing how to swim! It was a real struggle," she says. Immaculate shows scars of her boils, a whole year later.

They were stuck in the water for a long time, returning home only at 4 pm. Many men and women were taken away and jailed, recalls Mary.

Her voice rises in indignation as she tells us that some policemen entered the Lourdes church and urinated on the stage. They tried to burn the *pandal* and even broke Mother Mary's statue, she claims. These police excesses are corroborated by several people in Idinthakarai.

"We coastal people don't know much about peaceful means; we are rough and tough by nature and believe that we should be brave. If even our neighbours fight with us, we are ready to retaliate with weapons," says Mary candidly. "But in this struggle, things were different—even when the police harmed us, all we did was throw sand at them. We did not retaliate with any weapon."

The non-violent approach is credited to 'Uday Kumar Sir' who the women treat with great reverence. Mary defends him stoutly against government accusations of instigating villagers to protest against the plant. It is a common refrain in these parts, the answer anticipated and given even before the question can be asked: "Uday Sir became our leader because *we* wanted it, he himself did not make us do anything. He is part of the people and so he wants to save us. And we are not giving him bags of goods for his services, neither is he or any other leader benefited monetarily. All the work they are doing is so that people are disease-free with clean water, pure air and non-radiated fresh food to eat and live."

The non-violent image of the agitation was however adversely impacted by the events of September 10, 2012, which mainstream media like *The Indian Express* termed an"ugly turn" to a year-long peaceful struggle with "sporadic violence after police *lathi*-charged and burst tear gas shells to disperse over 2,000 protestors fighting pitched battles throwing stones and logs".

The paper also reported "enraged groups of protestors setting fire to a local panchayat office, the village administrative officer's office and a state-run liquor retail shop in Koodankulam". The rest of the English language press by and large reported similar versions, in some cases quoting the same press release-- "of the agitation turning violent with the death of a 44-year-old fisherman Anthony John in police firing in neighbouring Tuticorin district", "of 500 people stopping a train by squatting on the tracks and protestors blocking the Tuticorin-Nagercoil highway".

Television channels headlined the story 'Koodankulam stir gets violent', presenting conflicting versions of the villagers and the police. NDTV's Chennai correspondent Sam Daniels, who has covered the anti-KKNPP struggle since its inception, provided television viewers with the police and protestors' versions.

In the police version, Daniels reported that more than 4,000 protestors, led mostly by women and children, attempted to march towards the plant and lay siege to it, breaching the existing prohibitory orders for the second consecutive day. The police claimed the protestors had attacked them, injuring 100 policemen and forcing them to use tear gas. The protestors denied the use of violence, claiming that the police had deliberately staged a law and order situation to fire the tear gas, injuring many. The presence of more than 4,000 armed security forces around the village made it very difficult to enter Idinthakarai, with roads cordoned off.

"By the time I reached Idinthakarai on the evening of September 10, after being stopped and checked many times by police cordons around the village, there were thousands of people gathered inside the church compound and *pandal*," recalls Daniels in a personal interview. They reported their experiences to him, took him around the church pointing to broken idols lying on the ground, scratches on the walls, marks of policemen "urinating", but, he says, he was cautious about reporting on sensitive issues linked to religion. There was tension in neighbouring Kanyakumari and Tuticorin districts too, Daniels says; fishermen went on a solidarity strike and stayed away from the sea.

In interviews given to Daniels on-camera, wailing women asked plaintively: "The police are supposed to protect us; if they behave like this, where are we supposed to go?"

Was the police response to the protestors disproportionate, given that women and children formed a major part of the crowd on the seashore that day, I ask. Does dissent in any form or shape warrant such punitive action by the state? Daniels replies that the police follow orders from their political masters and with the state government changing its stand post-March 19 and opposing the plant, they were only obeying orders. The police also alleged that PMANE leaders used women and children as a shield, he says. In his report, filed during the 2012 agitation, in a piece-to-camera Sam had in fact asked: "Is it right to criminalise ordinary citizens and charge them with sedition?"

Kalpana Sharma, senior journalist and member of the fact-finding team that visited Idinthakarai and other villages in September 2012 after the showdown, wrote a scathing article titled 'Is it a crime to question?' in *The Hindu* (September 29):

> *With these wounds (caused by lathi-charges and burns) has come the realisation that in a democracy, even a peaceful protest is not tolerated. The women are puzzled about this. What did we do wrong, they ask. Can we not ask questions? Why does no one listen to our questions and talk to us directly? Indeed, why does no one listen? You hear words like "misled", or "instigated" by representatives of the police, the government and the nuclear power establishment. What they are suggesting is that these women lack intelligence, that they are simpletons who can be "misled". It is assumed that if people are either poor or unlettered, they have no ability to understand "complex" issues. But for the women in Idinthakarai there is nothing complex about the problem they are facing. Their future has been tied to a technology that has been proven to have devastating consequences in the event of an accident. And an accident can occur from a natural disaster—like a tsunami about which they are well aware, as they were affected in 2004—or human error. No one can guarantee that there will never be a human error.*

The trigger for the confrontation on the morning of September 10, according to the protesting villagers, was the police warning to 8,000 (police sources in newspaper reports claim the number was around 4,000) people gathered on the seashore to disperse in 10 minutes or face police action. Protestors alleged that even before the countdown ended, tear gas shells were lobbed at them and the police moved towards the centre of the assembled crowds to separate the women and children—who were in the front—from the men. In the *lathi*-charge and tear gassing that followed, while a large number of men escaped into the sea, women and children, who were more vulnerable, threw sand at the policemen to save themselves. A total of 66 people were arrested on that day including Xavier, Sundari, Selvi, Rose and Louduswamy.

The same day, allege villagers, at least 400 police persons entered the village of Idinthakarai and conducted door-to-door searches for the men; it was at this time that the police desecrated the Mother Mary shrine (breaking idols, spitting and urinating inside the church), pulling down tents where the protestors sit, destroying lights and water cans. As reported later in the report submitted by the fact-finding team of Kalpana Sharma, B G Kolse and Joe D'Cruz study:

> *Door-to-door searches were carried out in Tsunami Colony and Koodankulam village also where 65 people were arrested. The charges were the same in most cases irrespective of the age of the person arrested; four young boys between the ages of 15-16 were sent to the Pallayamkottai Juvenile Home; elderly men of 63, even 75 years, were arrested on charges of sedition and waging war against the state.*

Even as PMANE coordinator Uday Kumar and other leaders prepared to surrender to the police that was searching for them in order to protect the villagers from further harassment, emotional, tearful villagers stopped them from doing so. They all insisted on courting arrest. India Against Corruption activist Arvind Kejriwal (now Aam Aadmi Party chief), who arrived in Idinthakarai to express his support, endorsed the villagers' view. Ordinary people should have a say in what happens to them, said Kejriwal to the press, demanding a public debate on the Koodankulam issue.

While the world outside reacted with shock, and statements of solidarity from people like Mahashweta Devi, Aruna Roy, Lalita and Admiral Ramdas, PUCL, Tamil Nadu, were published in the newspapers, Idinthakarai continued to be virtually locked-down. Villagers report that essential supplies were blocked, water supply, electricity connections and communication lines cut off (in five adjoining villages, not just Idinthakarai).People injured in the melee were too scared to venture out for medical help. It was a long time before the situation returned to normal.

"The roads were blocked. They cut off all our supplies like water, milk and electricity," says Xavier Amma, eyes flashing at the memory. "We had to feed our small children sugar water instead of milk. The media felt bad for us so they brought us milk powder. We were provided with food through the coastal villages."

For Xavier Amma, quick-witted and intelligent, with arguably the loudest voice and widest smile in the village, what hurt most and lingers longest is the unwarranted shame of her 82-day incarceration in Trichy jail. She sees her arrest and jail term as a tactic by the government to isolate and make an example of her to dissuade other women from protesting. Xavier, like Mary and Sundari, is a well-travelled leader who has participated in rallies in Delhi, Kolkata, Bangalore, Coimbatore and Madurai, among other places.

The most haunting and immediate recall of Xavier Amma, however, is a photograph of the September 10, 2012 showdown at Idinthakarai beach. The frame shows a wailing Xavier with dishevelled hair lying prostrate at the edge of the water, unable to get up, arm flung upwards asking for help while several khaki-clad policemen circle the beach behind her.

Xavier recounts the exchange of hostilities in minute detail, her voice resonating with anger: "We were protesting near the plant on the seashore because we had heard that uranium was going to be filled in the plant which would be bad for the people. We did not try to destroy either the plant or any police van or hurt anyone; we were only protesting. The collector arrived there and told us to leave because we were protesting near the plant. We said we would not unless they stopped filling the uranium. They then asked for Uday Kumar but we told them to speak to us since we were the ones protesting. The collector asked five women to speak and so five of us asked him why we were being stopped from protesting on our own seashore. Even as we spoke, stones were thrown at us and the riot began. Even children were not spared and were tear-gassed. The children started running away but we women did not budge. The gas entered our noses. I felt suffocated and fell into the water and could not get up. Later two policemen lifted me up and two policewomen took me away. I was arrested at 11 am, held all day and taken to jail in Valliyur much later. No one in the village knew that I had been arrested. I was then presented in court and taken to Trichy jail. They filed six cases against me, saying I (and others) threw country bombs and bottles and destroyed a police van. We were taken far away so we wouldn't be here to protest. Since we had been so active in leading the protests, even travelling outside Idinthakarai to do so, they thought if they punished us it would scare the other women," says Xavier analysing the events.

For Xavier, the most galling aspect of her encounter with the punitive arm of the state—jails and courts, policemen and lawyers—was being treated as a common criminal and paraded as one. "We (Sundari, Selvi and I) were stripped and searched when we entered the gates of Trichy jail. We had never seen women stripping women before and felt extremely insulted and hurt. Then they took us into the jail room and repeated the process. Whenever the police had to take us to court by bus, everybody would stare at us at the bus stop which was humiliating; we felt ashamed. We had not stolen anything,we had not killed anyone, so when they transported us like criminals we felt terrible! It used to be a long ride by bus but they would not let us go to the toilet; they would go themselves but not allow us, saying they had to scan us first. They would let us use the toilet only once we reached court. In court they would say insulting things in front of so many people. My children too were not allowed to meet me in jail."

All of this however served to harden her resolve and Xavier emerged from jail "with guts to fight, not be afraid". We want our children to have happy, carefree lives, she says determinedly.We will protest till they stop the plant; it doesn't matter whether it takes 10 days or 10 years.

Gesturing to the roof of the *pandal* she reveals that it has been built for the second time in as many years. "No matter how many times we have to rebuild it, we will continue our protest. We protest as if it is our home; it has *become* our home," she says with a note of finality.

Xavier's daily schedule differs slightly from that of the other women. Along with a few select women, she also sleeps at the *pandal*, clocking an energetic roster of activities. She rattles them off quickly: "We sleep here at night, get up at 5 am for the Mass in church, go home, do the daily chores and cook for the children—

they eat on their own—and by 10 am we come here to protest. At 4 pm we listen to Uday Kumar's speech and then go home, eat dinner and return to the *pandal* at 7 to sleep."

Amal Raj clarifies the continuance of a practice that began in September 2012. "When the police entered Idinthakarai (post the September 10 clash on the seashore) and began arresting protestors, there were nearly 10,000 people sleeping here to protect themselves from arrest and to also protect Uday and Pushparyan. At that time there used to be power cuts for 17-18 hours so people slept here to be safe. Today people are more confident so only a few people sleep around the church every day."

Removing her round glasses and wiping the afternoon sweat off her forehead, Xavier comments wryly: "We were in a jail with bars all around us; our people were being harassed in a jail without bars."

Her compatriot in jail, the stocky and equally articulate Sundari, belongs to Perumanal village and shifted to Idinthakarai only after her marriage. Today, by her own admission she is an 'important person' in the village, representing it while talking to the media, to industrialists, to collectors. She uses her innate sense of humour even while describing grim occasions. "The police threw tear gas at us on September 10 when five of us (women) were talking to the collector and other officials. Children started fleeing to protect themselves but I did not know where my two children were. Even as I was talking to the officials, they realised I was an important person and took me away. I spent 98 days in jail with 78 charges against me including allegations that I had made country bombs, talked derogatorily about the chief minister and prime minister, propagated violence, was a traitor to the nation, and a lot more.

"On the 80th day they charged me with kidnapping the Tirunelveli collector. When they took me to court and announced this charge of kidnapping I couldn't control my laughter. I asked them: 'How can a simple woman who makes *beedis* and sells pickles for a living kidnap a government official? I don't have a huge gang! And if an official does not have protection in this nation then how can a common man have?' They couldn't answer my question. They told me I had committed a crime against the nation because I was protesting against something which the government had approved. I told them the government was initiated for the people and not the other way round. If they construct something in our home then they should ask if it is fine with us," she ends sarcastically.

Nobody can tell me not to protest, says Sundari fiercely, her firebrand personality on full display. She has compiled a book about her experiences in jail and sent it off for publication. "They harried us in jail, telling me there are 100 cases against me; that I would not see my children for the next seven to 10 years. They wanted me to sign a document saying I am protesting at the instigation of Uday Kumar, not on my own behalf. I told them: 'Uday Kumar may or may not be there tomorrow but I will protest for my children as they have to live on this land. And I will fight the cases filed against me'. The police would say things like 'a woman's job is to sleep with her husband and have children, not go around protesting'," says Sundari indignantly, adding that these are just a few of the incidents she has written about in her book.

Like Xavier, she was appalled and mortified at being strip-searched in jail; she was equally revolted at young female inmates being forced by the police to clear clogged septic tanks. She initiated protests against such treatment and also against the tasteless and inadequate food served at the jail, going on a three-day hunger strike to press her demands.

Threats and intimidation on a regular basis, says Sundari, have not stopped her from being among the first to volunteer for protest rallies; she sees herself as a role model for others in the village. "I get phone threats that my children's lives will be spoiled. But I am also treated as if I am the head of the women of Idinthakarai. I questioned the judge in court so the CID people asked me who had taught me how to speak to a judge. I answered: 'I am fighting against two governments, won't I know this much?'" she laughs.

Ruffling the hair of her two young children, eight and 10 years old, who have just joined her after morning school, Sundari gets emotional for the first time. "I don't feel the effects of the struggle, but my husband and children do. My children are scared that I will go back to jail so now whenever I go out they want to know where I am going. My husband has learnt how to cook! Initially my husband's family, even my siblings, did not agree with me and my stand but now I get respect," she says with pride.

Even outside Idinthakarai, says Sundari, people have started realising that there must be something wrong with KKNPP that protestors are willing to live away from their families, to be jailed for a cause. "People are scared of the police so they don't want to take part in the protests, because in big towns if someone is arrested even his neighbour will not be aware of it, so there is nobody to support you. But that does not mean people don't believe the plant is dangerous," she claims, speaking of her interaction with people in Madurai where she was kept during her 'conditional' bail period.

Allegations and complaints of continued police harassment, especially post-September 10, 2012, run rife not just in Idinthakarai but neighbouring Tsunami Colony, Vijaypathi and Koodankulam too.

Women huddled together for more than a month in front of the Lourdes church at the protest *pandal*, praying, protesting and keeping each other safe. Fifty-eight-year-old Parthimma lives in Tsunami Colony. She overruled the disapproval of her sons to station herself at Idinthakarai's *pandal* for a week, requesting her daughter to take care of her diabetic husband and the home. She shares her experiences with me frankly: "Of course I had to put up with a lot of difficulties to come here to protest, but I refused to budge. I am uneducated but even so I had gone to Chennai to participate in the protests. Sometimes we cannot even protest since the police block the western side of Idinthakarai with their vans." Her son was among those arrested after the clash between police and protestors in September. "For a whole month, the men in our village did not stay or sleep at home but went into hiding as the police would threaten us," says Parthimma. The entire colony was deserted, by the occupants' accounts.

Her Tsunami Colony neighbour Rani Kervin corroborates this: "The police would come to our homes and taunt us (women): 'Why are you here? Go there and protest!' At the September protests they would beat the men and drag them out like dogs; they don't treat us like human beings, they treat us like animals."

The non-fisher communities living in the village of Koodankulam less than 5 km from the plant also remain grimly obdurate after September 2012. Bala's husband Dharmatandi, a casual worker, was arrested in September on charges of sedition and involvement in the case of protestors setting fire to the panchayat office in Koodankulam."After 80 days in jail, he was released on conditional bail and would travel 300 km every Monday to sign in at the police station in Madurai; only recently has this procedure been transferred to the Koodankulam police station," she tells me.

Looking worn-out and resigned, 40-year-old Bala bemoans the fact that nobody helped her family when her husband was in jail. She had to sell her jewels to support her four children and handicapped aunt. She recalls the day her husband was dragged away by the police. "When the mayhem began my husband was asleep, so was my youngest son. Lots of policemen barged into our house, beat up my husband and took him away. In the melee I was pushed aside, my aunt was hurt and my small boy was hit on the head by a *lathi*. My husband was the sole earner in a household of seven, with four school-going children. After an agonising eight months, when my husband was released on bail he found it hard to get work because he had to sign in at the police station every Monday and the cases are still pending."

Though Bala has not personally attended protests against the plant at Idinthakarai, she declares that, like her, everyone in Koodankulam is against it: "Even though we are uneducated we have seen the Japan disaster on TV news. That scared us. We have struggled a lot in our lives and do not want our children to struggle. I want my four children to study hard, work and live happily without the fear of diseases like cancer. These will affect adults also, and as casual labourers we need to be fit," she says.

Repeating a common mantra, Bala adds: "We would rather die than leave our homes. We are fighting for our land and freedom. These outsiders put up a plant and electricity from that plant will benefit other states, yet we will be the victims of the resulting diseases. How is that fair? Only the government can provide justice. They can produce electricity through other ways, we don't want nuclear power."

Testimonies like these are the only known records of what people who live closest to a nuclear plant—*this* nuclear plant—feel, think and understand how it will affect their lives. These project-affected people (PAP), as they are collectively dubbed, have not provided their testimonies to expert committees appointed by the state and central governments to investigate safety, livelihood and environmental impact simply because they have not been visited or asked. Villagers deny meeting any officials at all; only civil society groups have recorded their side of the story.

Ten days after the clash between police and the protestors of Idinthakarai, a fact-finding team comprising former Bombay High Court judge B G Kolse, senior journalist Kalpana Sharma and Tamil writer R N JoeD'Cruz recorded the individual testimonies of people in Idinthakarai, Tsunami Colony, Vairavikinaru and Koodankulam. Their report, dated September 26, 2012, provides evidence of many people having been injured—burn injuries from tear gas shells that were fired, others from *lathi*-charges.

Excerpts from the fact-finding report:

> *Villagers complained about the desecration of the Lourdes Matha church, where the police reportedly broke an idol of Mother Mary and urinated inside the church premises. Broken pieces of the idol were shown to the team...*
>
> *In Tsunami Colony, the fear was palpable. Most houses were locked as people are afraid to return to their homes. Several villagers showed us their houses where windowpanes had been broken, cupboards ransacked and doors damaged allegedly by the police who entered the village on September 10. Thereafter*

for several days, a police force camped in the village. As a result even today many of the residents of the village are afraid to spend the night there and instead sleep in the tent outside the Lourdes Matha church in Idinthakarai.

Fear was also evident in Vairavikinaru village where villagers showed us evidence of the destruction to houses when the police party raided the village on September 10. Nine people were arrested including a 16-year-old boy and a 75-year-old man who is practically blind in one eye. The people we spoke to kept repeating that they did not know what they had done to invite such treatment from the police.

Villagers in Koodankulam are even more terrified as they live closest to the Koodankulam Nuclear Power Project. On September 10, a large police contingent entered the village, arrested 34 people, broke into houses where the frightened residents hid, and destroyed property and vehicles. Now, villagers said they are so afraid that they lock their doors after dark, many cannot sleep and are fearful when they hear a vehicle entering the village.

In all these villages, one common factor was that each of those arrested was charged under identical sections. These included 124A (sedition), 121A (waging war against the state), 307, 353 and 147 and 148.

The other more disturbing testimony was from the women in all four villages. They spoke of the abusive and sexist remarks of the police when they came to their village and also when some of the women went to the police station. One disabled woman gave evidence of physical molestation and another, who was part of the protest on the beach near the plant, spoke of police chasing the women into the sea and making obscene gestures.

> *Despite this situation, villagers expressed their determi-nation to oppose the project. However, they repeatedly asked why no one from the government or from the Nuclear Power Corporation of India Limited was prepared to hold a proper public hearing where they heard the apprehensions of the villagers and presented their point of view. They asserted that as the people living closest to the nuclear plant they had a right to question and to know all the facts.*

Of the many heart-rending testimonies mentioned in the fact-finding report, Idinthakarai's 43-year-old Ritamma's parting comments encapsulate the overwhelming fear that haunts every person living near KKNPP:

> *Ritamma, 43, was hit on the bridge of her nose by a lathi. She said:*

> *"On the 10th morning, Jeyakumar, our parish priest came to us and told us to disperse. He said he would talk to the police and work for a consensus. As we were talking to him, the SP announced that we needed to disperse in 10 minutes. Even as we were trying to decide what has to be done, we heard some noise on the right side and police were attacking a bunch of youngsters who were in volunteer clothes. I saw my son in that crowd and ran there to protect him. I felt a strong blow on my face and a lathi tore my nose. We ran and the police chased us and they would not even leave the men who jumped into the sea. They were throwing teargas shells at men who were in the water.*

> *If we cannot protest peacefully today against KKNPP on our own soil in our own village, what will happen to us once they start this nuclear plant? If they don't listen to our fears today, how are we to believe that they will be there when we get affected?"*

Recalling her visit to Idinthakarai and neighbouring villages in September 2012, Kalpana tells me how moving it was to see the people's determination to continue to resist despite all the difficulties they had faced. "The Tamil Nadu police charged those arrested under Section 124A (sedition) and 121A (waging war against the state). This was designed to suppress the movement. They clearly hoped that such charges would frighten the people into giving up. But as we saw when we went to the area, far from being discouraged, people were even more determined to continue their fight. In the long run however, the use of these provisions in the law will strike at the very root of dissent in this country. It leaves no space for honest debate, for questioning, for people to demand that they be heard."

On September 13, 2012, more than 3,000 villagers including PMANE leaders, women and children of Idinthakarai stepped into the sea once again, holding hands and forming a human chain in a *jal satyagraha* from 10 am till the sun set. Once again, the protestors flouted prohibitory orders, waving black flags, their boats tied to the shore. The low aerial surveillance runs conducted by the coastguard caught 38-year-old Sahyam Francis unawares; he lost his balance and fell into the water, hitting his head, according to eyewitness reports by villagers. He died later in hospital. The entire village attended his funeral and took an oath to stop the commissioning of the plant. Graveyard protests to seek the help of their ancestors was another form of agitation that continued even as the Supreme Court turned down the Special Leave Petition filed by the movement's legal team asking for yet another stay on uranium fuel loading at the plant.

On September 16, 2012 in a powerful visual image, protestors in Koottapuli buried themselves up to their necks in sand near a graveyard, with the first few rows comprising children. Their explanation to the media gathered at the site was straightforward: "If the plant starts it will be death for us, like being buried, so we are doing this."

The state continued to assert that the Koodankulam plant was safe, that nuclear energy was clean and cheap energy and that there was full compliance with all safety norms. Chief Minister Jayalalitha, Environment Minister Jayanti Natarajan and Home Minister Sushil Shinde issued statements to this effect in quick succession.

On September 21, 2012, uranium fuel was loaded at KKNPP.

~

The anti-KKNPP movement continued its agitations.

A peaceful boat siege was held on October 8 with a list of demands that included the release of all arrested, withdrawal of the police from villages to facilitate a return to normalcy, and, as always, closure of the plant.

On October 29, they laid siege to the Tamil Nadu Legislative Assembly building. In November they marched in procession to Thomaiyyarpuram to celebrate World Fisheries Day. World Human Rights Day and the sombre anniversaries of the Bhopal gas tragedy and tsunami were also observed before bringing in the new year with a three-day festival of music, films and discussions with activists from all over the country. Groups from West Bengal, Jharkhand, Chhattisgarh, Uttar Pradesh and Delhi, including activists Dr Binayak Sen, Prashant Bhushan and Admiral (retd) Ramdas spent new year's eve with the people of Idinthakarai and 'saluted their valiant struggle'.

Seven months after uranium fuel was loaded at the plant, with the plant still not in operation, India's atomic energy regulator AERB issued a statement that four defective valves were being replaced at the first unit and that clearance for the plant would be granted only after a satisfactory review.

On May 6, 2013, the Supreme Court rejected a petition filed by G Sundar Rajan (repeating the concerns of non-compliance with 17 safety recommendations and the flouting of other norms). The court cleared the commissioning of the Koodankulam plant, declaring it safe and secure and necessary for the larger public interest and economic growth of the country. While setting out 15 guidelines for AERB to follow regarding commissioning, safety, security and environmental issues, the court observed that nuclear power plants are needed in India for present and future generations.

The PMANE struggle committee met with community leaders of all the affected villages to plan a new course of action. Their legal and environmental teams held discussions and press conferences to express their rejection of the Supreme Court judgment.

The fiery Sundari tells me a story that best illustrates the villagers' conviction that with god on their side, they would prevail. "A corner of our huge roof at the Samara *pandal*—which was due for repairs—collapsed one day. Nobody was hurt since it happened at 3 pm and nobody was sitting in the area. The women were praying in the church foyer. If it had happened a little later or earlier, when school closes for the day and lots of children cross the *pandal*, it would have resulted in tragedy. That day everyone said god is with us."

Chapter Five

CHINKS IN THE KOODANKULAM ARMOUR

June 2013

The tiny drawing-room of Tamilarasi's home in Tsunami Colony barely leaves room for the two of us to sit on two cane chairs and talk about the Koodankulam nuclear plant that is less than a kilometre away. An hour goes by and Tamilarasi brings biscuits and tea, apologising that there is no milk. A sudden shriek and joyous clapping by her 14-year-old daughter Luvasana-the student who stood up to the Tirunelveli collector-prompts her mother to explain, "We have had no power for five days and it has just come back on, so she is happy!"

She goes on to state the obvious irony—"We are the ones who need the power most but not nuclear power from Koodankulam".

July 2013

Comfortably ensconced on reclining chairs in a spacious and beautiful living room in a posh apartment in Mumbai, my friend Alpana and I catch up on each others' lives over afternoon tea. After some time I casually mention that the Koodankulam nuclear reactor in Tamil Nadu has just gone critical and she replies enthusiastically, "Yes, isn't that great?" Alpana is a former journalist; well-read, well-

informed and well-off.

I am curious about her ringing endorsement of the Koodankulam plant and ask her why she supports it. "Well, I don't know much about the politics of the Koodankulam plant," she answers, back-tracking a little, "and in general people aren't concerned about nuclear power, but there aren't too many options are there? So why not, if it doesn't cause any damage-and there is no immediate damage, it is potential damage, which most people can't comprehend," she reasons.

According to PMANE leaders and supporters of the anti-KKNPP movement, if there is an accident at the Koodankulam power plant, it will possibly affect 10 districts in South India—Madurai, Viruthunagar, Thoothukudi, Tirunelveli, Kanyakumari districts in Tamil Nadu and Thiruvananthapuram, Kollam, Pathanamthitta, Alapuzha and Kottayam districts in Kerala. For the rest of the country—barring anti-nuke activists and some concerned citizens—Koodankulam would be hard to find on a map, harder to pronounce and hardest to relate to in any meaningful way. Nuclear power and its inherent advantages or disadvantages does not figure anywhere in the daily lives of the average Indian citizen; at best it may be a fleeting thought in the minds of the residents of Tamil Nadu when faced with an electricity cut/outage.

For those living with a nuclear plant in their backyard, the reality is starkly different. *Kathirveechu* (Tamil for radiation) is a fear that dominates their lives and dictates their choices —to protest, to fast, to demonstrate against the government, to walk long distances, to face arrest and incarceration. *Nobody* believes the government's assurances that the plant is totally safe. The government has, according to them, made several promises about the plant; not one has been honoured over the last 25 years.

A year after work on the Koodankulam plant began in 1988, *The Illustrated Weekly of India* correspondent K P Sunil travelled to the area, in March 1989, to talk to villagers and report on resistance already mounting against the plant. Excerpts from his article, twenty four years ago, illustrate how palpable the fears of the project-affected were even then, how strong their resistance, and how little has changed in the years since:

> *"Ten years ago the surveyors who came here told us they were going to build a naval base and harbour here. Only later did they say that an atomic plant was to be put here. They said that there was nothing to worry as the government and the authorities of the plant would always be around to help in the event of any emergency.*

> *In 1979 a cyclone struck this coast. Around 8 o'clock at night the radio news said that everybody in this area had to move to safer places. I had a small baby in my arms. And my old mother-in-law. I had to trudge with them several miles on foot in pouring rain. No government came to our help. Is that government going to take us away in aeroplanes if the atomic reactors burst? Let that fellow (Rajiv Gandhi) send his army here. Let them shoot us all dead as they are doing in Sri Lanka. And then let them build their nuclear plant over our dead bodies."—Lema Navarez, housewife from Koodankulam village*

> *"I am fighting the nuclear plant purely on humanitarian grounds. Nuclear projects are something our country can well do without. For every positive reason in favour of the plant there are a hundred negative factors to more than adequately neutralise it. For 25 years of power-generation we have to guard a veritable atom bomb for 25,000 years. For providing employment to a few hundred qualified personnel, tens of thousands of poor people who*

have lived in this area for years will have to be driven off from their sole means of livelihood, be it agriculture or fishing."— Idinthakarai's parish priest Father Iruthayaraj

Says Paul Navarez, an outspoken member of the fishermen's community working with the merchant navy, on shore leave: "What we dread the most is the effect of radiation on future generations. They say that accidents will not occur. And that even if they occur steps will be taken to minimise the effects. Then they say that as soon as the announcement is made people should rush into their houses and close all the doors and windows to prevent the radiation from entering in. Most people in villages live in huts, doors and windows are mere openings with no shutters. The ceilings and walls have holes and cracks. So what do they do? How can they protect themselves from the radiation?

"As if this were not enough, they say that rescue operations will be conducted by the authorities by hiring a fleet of 200-300 buses from local operators. Now we once hired seven buses to take people of this village from here to Tirunelveli to stage a protest demonstration. And on that occasion we learnt how difficult it was to arrange just seven buses. And we have to depend on rescue operations to be conducted in hired buses! By the time the buses arrive there will be very little of the village left."

"The government thinks people are fools," puts in Iruthayaraj. "They have become so accustomed to imposing their will on the people that they think we will keep on nodding our heads like Tanjore dolls always. But for everything there is a limit."

"...The women here will not allow the atomic power station to come up. We will protest. And we are prepared even to go up to the prime minister. If after all this, they still persist in their *mad design, every one of the women here will jump into the trenches they will dig for laying the foundation. Let them build the reactor on our samadhis! Instead of killing us and our future generations cell by cell, we will all perish in one day."—Matilda, schoolteacher, Koodankulam*

Twenty-four years later, sitting at the Samara *pandal* in Idinthakarai where he is a regular, 57-year-old Rajalingam sets aside the Tamil daily *Dinamani* and encapsulates two decades of personal history in an hour. Rajalingam is relatively well-off, having worked in the Gulf earlier; he was also a farmer and owned land in Koodankulam which was bought by NPCIL. He says that since the land was in his grandfather's name and he did not have the relevant documents he received no money for it. "The government did not ask the consent of the people, and the people did not oppose it either. Those whose lands were in their own names got their money (paltry sums of Rs 2,000 per acre) and those who didn't could not afford to go to court to claim the money deposited there by the government. Of the total 3,800 acres (1,538 hectares) that was taken, only 50% of people received the money," he claims.

Uday agrees that several legal cases continue to be fought in Koodankulam with respect to the land acquisition compensation and cites paucity of time and manpower for PMANE's inability to help villagers in this regard.

According to NPCIL's own data, it acquired 929 hectares for the project and 150 hectares for the township, in the late-1980s. A later report in the Supreme Court cites the total land acquired by NPCIL as 1,225 hectares, between 1991-93, with no displacement of people and a total compensation of Rs 62,02,332 given to the people of Koodankulam. The land acquired for Units 1 and 2 was earmarked for four more reactors, leading to further protests by villagers.

People were also denied permission to construct houses at the time, says Rajalingam, since the area was being cleared for the plant. As the number of people wanting to build houses increased, word spread and everyone became aware that the promise of setting up a factory was a sham, he adds. The expected jobs for locals did not materialise, except for a small percentage in the semi-skilled and labour categories. On paper, according to NPCIL's expert group report on Koodankulam: "Only land-losers who are displaced as a result of land acquisition by public sector undertakings are to be given priority in jobs." Since NPCIL says there was no displacement of families due to land acquisition, this did not apply. There are records of 541 employees recruited, 528 from Tamil Nadu in Group B, C and D category jobs, while 2,000-3,000 locals were employed with contractors. There is no reference by NPCIL to the promise of one job per family for those selling land for the KKNPP project, though people's expectations regarding the same are clearly referred to in official documents.

Koodankulam's 20,000-strong population (as calculated by residents in 2013 and reported in the media; the 2011 census records a population of 12,957) comprises farmers, masons, labourers, beedi-makers, shop and small business owners. "Radiation will harm everyone, not just fisherfolk. Livestock like cows and goats, our produce like pulses will be affected; so will agriculture. People will not buy our agricultural produce since it is cultivated within 30 km of the plant. So we will all be affected," declares Rajalingam.

Rajalingam has not returned to Koodankulam since September 10, 2012. His house is searched regularly, a police van is always stationed outside, there are more than 100 cases of sedition against him, he says. "I am not a hooligan or a traitor. I don't drink or smoke. People respect me. The police have no reason to arrest me other than the fact that I protest and gather people for the protests."

He continues with the now-familiar refrain: "I will be here till they close the plant. So what if it takes a long time? I have lived my life but I want my children and the next generations to be happy. This land and sea should be protected. Many people have protested in this country, like Mahatma Gandhi. We are protesting in a non-violent way, which does not bother the government. We have not asked the government for anything. The police or the court cases do not scare us. The government does not follow its own rules, the kilometre restriction for example. There is supposed to be a 10,000 population limit within a 5-km radius of the plant but there are 50,000 people within 5 km," he asserts.

Rajalingam scoffs at the listed benefits of nuclear energy in sections of the media, pointing to alternative ways of producing 'current', like solar, wind, tides or biogas. The cost of protecting the plant for so many years would be very high, he analyses. As for disaster management, he points to an article in the day's newspaper and says: "They could not deal with the Uttarakhand flood situation; if the meteorological department had calculated properly, so many lives could have been saved. And you expect them to save us in a nuclear disaster?"

An uneducated villager from Koodankulam, Rajalingam has in one short outburst, highlighted key issues linked to the plant as well as the government's dismissive attitude towards the PAP (project-affected people). On a more personal note, he acknowledges the toll his exile has taken on his family: "When the man of the house is not able to work, it affects the family; if he is not there at all, it affects the family psychologically. They cry when they call me," he ends sadly.

Less than 6 km away, in Koodankulam village, Rajalingam's son-in-law Tamilselvam, a self-employed 29-year-old computer engineer points to the plant, visible at a distance from the terrace of his house, saying: "If that plant were not there, we would have a very peaceful life here. In the last 10 years Koodankulam has developed a lot compared to the other villages. But if the plant is started, our life will always be in a shadow; we will always fear accidents because the quality of the materials used in the plant is not good. I don't trust them; I used to work there in 2004 as a supervisor in the erection field but quit after a month because they did not believe me when I pointed out a flaw."

Driving through the narrow lanes of Koodankulam which looks like any other village in Tamil Nadu, the only difference I perceive is an air of caution. The Idinthakarai car driver refuses to wait for me in Koodankulam; he also flatly refuses to drive anywhere near the plant for me to get even the most cursory glimpse, telling me that the Koodankulam police station is right opposite the plant and he didn't want to risk going anywhere near it. I also find most people reluctant to give interviews about the nuclear plant, preferring to congregate at one place, seeking safety in numbers.

Eighty percent of the population in Koodankulam is against the plant, says Tamilselvam who fully supports the protests at Idinthakarai and other places. He adds scornfully that, in June 2012, NPCIL provided information and guidelines on what to do in case of an accident only to the 200 people living in the village of Nakkaneri, 5 km away.

Power from windmills and solar power are alternatives to nuclear power, Tamilselvam explains. There are around 1,000 windmills in the Koodankulam and Tirunelveli area, he estimates, and eight windmills inside the KKNPP complex! For eight months in a year, the wind is strong and can be harnessed. The existing windmills are private ones, each operating at 1.2 MWe, costing approximately Rs 6 crore, plus a subsidiary amount from the government. Even a thousand windmills would be a fraction of the cost of a nuclear plant, he says, adding that the area has infrequent rain so solar power is another viable option.

Ruing the fact that the name Koodankulam has become synonymous with agitation, linked to a certain notoriety, he says simply: "We don't want a name, we want to live."

Tamilselvam, Rajalingam, Amal Raj and of course the indomitable women Xavier Amma, Sundari, Mary, Milret, Tamilarasi to name just a few among scores of other protesting project-affected people—are not only aware of but also remarkably articulate about existing guidelines and rules related to KKNPP and the "wrongs" committed by NPCIL at various stages of the plant's design, production, construction, environment assessment and disaster management. This easily contradicts the government's stance that the villagers would find it difficult to understand the technicalities involved in a nuclear power plant. In fact, the villagers' primary grievance against the authorities—be it government expert committees or NPCIL or even Dr Abdul Kalam who visited the plant in 2011—is that no one cared enough to talk to them before taking a decision that would impact and change *their* lives the most.

"It is indeed true that we live in a society of risky choices, but it is one in which only some do the choosing while others do the risking," the quote by Slovenian philosopher Slavoj Zizek in nuclear physicist M V Ramana's book, *The Power of Promise: Examining Nuclear Energy in India* is an accurate reflection of the sentiments of lakhs of project-affected people. In village after village, home after home, discussion after discussion, the response to government's claims of KKNPP being absolutely safe was the same: "Why don't scientists and ministers build a home in Idinthakarai or Tsunami Colony and live there to show that the plant is a hundred percent safe?" For all those who term their reactions purely emotional, unfounded in science or empirical knowledge, the villagers unleash a further volley of questions, a majority of which remain unanswered.

Why did it take 24 years for KKNPP to be commissioned in July 2013? Why have none of the people living near the plant been consulted, informed or warned about trials (hot runs and their effects), disaster management plans including evacuation or rehabilitation? Which hospital are they supposed to go to for treatment in case of accident, injury or illness related to the plant? If the waste water—even low-level waste—discharged into the sea from the plant alters water temperatures and adversely impacts marine life and fish catch, how will fisherfolk survive? How much electricity *will* the plant produce, and how will it be cheaper? Who will benefit from this power; will it primarily benefit the villagers living adjacent to the plant or will large corporations and companies in the cities be the primary beneficiaries? Can the government provide a hundred percent guarantee that a Fukushima-type disaster will never take place at the Koodankulam plant? Can they guarantee that an earthquake or tsunami like the one in 2004 will not happen again in this area? Can anyone guarantee that there is no terrorist threat to a nuclear facility?

It does not take long to discover that sharing information—with PAP, the media (except in select, chosen circumstances), writers, activists and of course anti-KKNPP protestors—is not a priority for all agencies involved in the decision-making process. The chain of command goes like this—the NPCIL reports to the Department of Atomic Energy, whose secretary chairs the Atomic Energy Commission that AERB reports to! None of them like to share information with the public.

Despite government efforts to "allay the people's fears" about the Koodankulam plant post-Fukushima by setting up central and state expert teams to investigate the safety of KKNPP, and appointing a Government of India task force that submitted its findings on the plant in May 2011, the trust deficit remains unchanged. The expert teams did not meet project-affected people, causing further resentment. As for the task force's report: 11 of the 17 safety recommendations for the reactor made to AERB were overlooked by it and initial fuel loading started in August 2012 regardless.

After images of the Fukushima disaster in March 2011 were telecast in the homes of villagers of Idinthakarai, Koodankulam, Vairavikinaru and other villages near the plant, it wasn't just PMANE that called for a moratorium on further activity at the plant. In an open letter, eminent citizens such as social scientists Romila Thapar, Ramachandra Guha and Jean Dreze, dancers Leela Samson and Malavika Sarukkai, former bureaucrats/diplomats SP Shukla, Nirupam Sen and EAS Sarma, retired navy chief L Ramdas, writers Arundhati Roy and Nayantara Sahgal, scientists MV Ramana and PM Bhargava, artists Krishen Khanna and Vivan Sundaram, and former vice-chancellors Mushirul Hasan and Deepak Nayyar, advocated "an independent, transparent safety audit of all of India's nuclear facilities, which involves non-DAE experts and civil society organisations".

This proposal, stated by Dr Balaram, director of the Indian Institute of Science and a member of Prime Minister Manmohan Singh's scientific advisory council, suggested that "in light of what has happened in Japan... we strongly believe that India must radically review its nuclear power policy for appropriateness, safety, costs, and public acceptance. Pending the review, there should be a moratorium on all further nuclear activity, and revocation of recent clearances for nuclear projects". This independent review did not take place then or later.

In November 2011, former President Dr Abdul Kalam visited the Koodankulam plant and pronounced it completely safe. In an interview published in *The Hindu*, he said: "I am completely satisfied and happy with the sophisticated safety features of the reactors and hence there is no need for panic since it's only a boon to the future generation." No tsunami or earthquake would affect the reactors, he claimed; no waste from the reactor would be dumped into the sea. He suggested creating a nuclear safety institute in the Koodankulam area for continued research into the safety aspects of coast-based nuclear power plants in India and abroad. "Nuclear scientists have to interact with people and academic institutions continuously to update nuclear power-generation technology and safety." He predicted that the Koodankulam area would be known to the world in another 10 years as the "greatest nuclear power complex in a single area".

The people living in this area however did not get the opportunity to share their views and fears about the nuclear complex, or discuss the plant's safety with him. And neither did I, almost two years later.

A formal request for an interview with Dr Kalam in August 2013 was turned down with the advisory that I "may refer to the article written by Dr Kalam and published by *The Hindu* in November 2011" and that "he would not be in a position to comment anything on this issue now".

In an essay titled 'Nuclear power is our gateway to a prosperous future', published in *The Hindu* on November 6, 2011, Dr Kalam listed key reasons for promoting nuclear power in India. The article elicited a lot of feedback from readers, evenly divided between praise and scepticism:

> *Today, India finds itself going through a phase of rapid ascent in economic empowerment. Industries are evolving at a significantly higher rate since liberalisation. Our focus for this decade will be on the development of key infrastructure and the uplifting of the 600,000 villages where 750 million people live, as vibrant engines of the economy.*
>
> *It is predicted that the total electricity demand will grow from the current 150,000 MW to at least over 950,000 MW by the year 2030...*
>
> *...The greenest sources of power are definitely solar and wind. With abundant sunshine and places of high wind velocity, the nation definitely has potential for these forms of energy. But solar and wind power, despite all their advantages, are not stable and are dependent excessively on weather and sunshine conditions. Nuclear power, on the other hand, provides a relatively clean, high-density source of reliable energy with an international presence. Today, there are 29 countries operating 441 nuclear power plants, with a total capacity of about 375 GW(e)...*
>
> *...Meanwhile in India, we are not generating even 5,000 MW of*

nuclear power from the total of about 150 GW of electricity-generation, most of it coming from coal...

...So, will we allow an accident in Japan, in a 40-year-old reactor at Fukushima, arising out of extreme natural stresses, to derail our dreams to be an economically developed nation?...

...In 1903, the Wright brothers translated into reality the remarkable dream of controlled human flight. Not more than half a decade later, in 1908, the first flight disaster occurred, which severely injured Orville Wright and killed his co-passenger. Many accidents followed, and even today air accidents kill more than 1,500 people every year. Imagine whether we would be flying between distant cities, across oceans and continents, if the incident of 1908, or the ones later, were used as a reason to disband human flight?...

...Affordable, clean and abundant energy provided by nuclear sources is our gateway to a future that is healthy, learned and connected.

Partly in response to Dr Kalam's public endorsement of nuclear power in general and KKNPP in particular, in November 2011, and partly to address questions encountered in the course of their street and college campaigns, the Chennai Solidarity Group for Koodankulam Struggle brought out a factsheet, a ready reckoner on nuclear power and Koodankulam. Excerpts from the factsheet authored by Nityanand Jayaraman and G Sundar Rajan:

In more than 60 years of post-Independence industrialisation and modernisation, the contribution of nuclear energy to the total electricity-generation is less than 3%. Renewable energy sources already contribute more than 10% of India's electricity...

...The path to a sustainable and socially just future lies in moving

away from environmentally destructive technologies such as coal and nuclear. Nuclear energy will not help us combat climate change. Per unit of power, nuclear energy emits four to five times more carbon dioxide (CO_2) than renewable energy...

...Besides the better known disasters at Kyshtym, in erstwhile USSR (1957), Three Mile Island (1979) and Chernobyl (1986), at least 76 nuclear accidents totalling $19.1 billion in damages have occurred between 1947 and 2008. Most of these accidents—56 to be precise—happened after the Chernobyl disaster. This translates to one serious nuclear incident every year causing $332 million in damages annually.

And it is not just disasters that we are concerned about. Even nuclear reactors that "operate perfectly" are associated with higher risks of cancer and unexplained deaths. In the US, where 104 reactors are operating at 65 sites, elevated rates of leukemia and brain cancers are reported from communities near nuclear power plants.

Consider the costs of a disaster. Belarus, a state in the erstwhile USSR, suffered the maximum damage as a result of the 1986 Chernobyl nuclear disaster. According to a report by the International Atomic Energy Agency, between 1991 and 2003, Belarus spent $13 billion on disaster-related expenses. It has estimated its losses over 30 years at $235 billion. Radiation fallout from the disaster has contaminated more than 200,000 sq km, mostly in Russia, Belarus and Ukraine. That is about twice the size of Tamil Nadu...

...The argument against Koodankulam is not an argument against science and experimentation. Unwilling people cannot be asked to sacrifice their lives in the interest of Kalam's science. The people supporting the Koodankulam struggle are not 'Can't

Doers'; they are 'Won't Doers'. Dr Kalam is not talking about risking his life for the advancement of science; he is blaming the Koodankulam people for refusing to risk their lives.

If the Koodankulam plant is completely safe as Dr Kalam puts it, it would be useful to see Dr Kalam convincing the insurance companies to provide blanket cover to nuclear power plants, and convincing the nuclear equipment suppliers to abandon their insistence on a nuclear liability protocol that exempts them from compensating in the event of a disaster, even if it is caused by a willful fault on their part.

Building a nuclear plant merely on the basis of a belief—as if in god—that a tsunami or major earthquake will not occur is what is anti-science. People who are agitated and fearful of the consequences of the nuclear technology being set up in India are scientific because their fears are based on the empirical evidence of regular disasters and a knowledge of the socio-economic and environmental fall-outs of such disasters. The fear is further fuelled by the lack of transparency that shrouds nuclear establishments in India and elsewhere...

...Car accidents or even plane accidents do not leave behind a 20 km exclusion zone in which human life cannot return to normal for decades. A person driving in a car or travelling by plane accepts certain risks voluntarily. A car or a plane accident does not affect the next generation and the unborn.

Apprising project-affected people of the underlying factors and risks involved in the Koodankulam plant, consulting with them on the best course of action and backing joint decisions has been the PMANE mandate since its formation in 2001. The mandate is shared by supporters like the Chennai Solidarity Group for Koodankulam Struggle. The government calls this involvement with locals "misleading the villagers".

In the twenty four years since the Koodankulam nuclear deal was signed in 1988, the government has had ample opportunity to reassure those affected by the plant that it was safe, their livelihoods were safe, their future generations were safe. In the absence of any such reassurance or guarantee of protection and rehabilitation in case of a disaster, the people's apprehensions and mistrust multiplied ten-fold. Interminable delays in commissioning the plant fuelled further suspicion, and PMANE's persistent questions through RTI applications unearthed corruption and quality concerns.

The space for discussion and dialogue with locals—unused and unacknowledged by successive governments—was filled by PMANE leaders and activists who set up base in Idinthakarai from 2011. They went on to energise the villagers whose stand against the plant intensified after the Fukushima disaster.

The equally firm assertion by government, by pro-nuclear groups, by Dr Kalam that nuclear power is the clean, safe, cheap energy needed for India's future economic growth, and that the Koodankulam plant is totally safe is today dismissed outright by project-affected people. Their perception and their experience of the plant is their only reality, their only truth, and nobody has been able to change that in over two decades.

A litany of "transgressions" on the part of the plant's operators NPCIL as well as the government has only fuelled the volatile situation. PMANE activists have diligently brought these to the fore in their fight against the plant, starting with the date of commissioning (when the plant begins its operations or goes critical).

On November 26, 1988, Tamil Nadu Governor P C Alexander announced that he expected the Koodankulam project to be completed by 1998; Tamil Nadu would receive 28% of the power generated, the rest would go to the national grid. Twenty-three years later, on December 15, 2011, Prime Minister Manmohan Singh announced the commissioning of the plant "in a couple of weeks" during his Russia visit.

According to environmental journalist Nityanand Jayaraman, V Narayansamy, minister of state in the PMO, made 14 failed predictions about the plant's commissioning between October 2010 and October 2012. Nityanand stopped keeping track thereafter. "The postponements alarmed villagers, giving rise to fears of irregularities and improprieties associated with the plant," a PMANE press release pointed out.

Along with regular updates on the progress of the Koodankulam plant through press releases and online blogs, PMANE leaders, Uday Kumar in particular, have published handbooks that offer their perspective on the sins of omission or commission of what Uday calls "nukedom".

The first is site evaluation of the Koodankulam plant (Units 1 and 2), announced to have been completed in 1998: details of who did the evaluation, what was done, what strengths and weaknesses were identified, whether the evaluation was verified by an independent authority have never been provided.

No environmental impact assessment (EIA) has been done either, nor has a public hearing been held for Units 1 and 2. An EIA study is mandated for governmental projects such as nuclear plants and industries but it was formally introduced only in 1994, and by 1989 Units 1 and 2 of the Koodankulam plant had already received environmental clearance (EC). The existing laws provide that a clearance is valid for only five years after operation or construction (Koodankulam construction began in 2002). Moreover, there were enormous changes in the original plan on which the 1989 clearance was based, so a fresh EIA and public hearing should have been called for but was not done.

"For Units 1 and 2 there was no public hearing and no EIA (an EIA extrapolated from the one for Units 3 and 4 was provided later and is available on the NPCIL website). None of the guidelines were followed. That is the reason why NPCIL are hesitant to give a copy of the site evaluation and safety analysis report. When we asked for a copy of the EIA they said these environmental laws had not come (into existence) at the time so they haven't done any of them. So the EIA for 1 and 2 is kind of a grandfathered version of the EIA for Units 3 to 6," says Uday Kumar, adding: "It is a project affecting the people so *they* must have the last say, not the court or any other body. That is why we do EIAs and public hearings."

Villagers claim that the public hearing that did take place (after three postponements) for Units 3 and 4 of KKNPP, on June 2, 2007, was farcical. According to a report in Infochange (September 2011), approximately 7,000 people from three districts—Tirunelveli, Thoothukudi and Kanyakumari—attended the hearing held at the Government Engineering College in Tirunelveli, with 1,200 police personnel in riot gear in attendance. The EIA was not available in Tamil so many people did not understand the facts about radiation levels and its impact on the environment and livelihoods.Then the public hearing was halted abruptly, with the collector announcing that the villagers' questions had been satisfactorily answered by NPCIL.

The most visible violation of the AERB's own guidelines is

the rule about restricted zones of population. The exclusion zone is within 1.5 km from the nuclear plant; entry here is for restricted personnel only, no human habitation is allowed. The seclusion zone is up to 5 km from the plant, where a maximum of 20,000 people are allowed to reside. The emergency planning zone is a 16-km radius from the plant, while the 30-km radius requires a limit of 100,000 residents.

In direct contravention of these rules, the last house in Tsunami Colony is less than 1 km from the plant, and all 450 houses constructed there in 2006, with at least 4,000 people living in them, and constructed well after the plant was a reality, are within 1.5 km. According to PMANE calculations and media articles in *Sanhati*, *Dianuke* and *Kracktivist*, at least 40,000 people reside in the seclusion zone while approximately 10 lakh people live within the 30 km zone, making evacuation in case of a disaster virtually impossible.

In reply to an unstarred question raised in the Rajya Sabha, in December 2011, V Narayansamy, minister of state in the PMO said: "The population in the sterilised zone of (the) Koodankulam site at the time of site selection was 15,042. Koodankulam and Idinthakarai villages fall within the sterilised zone of the Koodankulam nuclear power plant. As per the 2001 census, the population in Koodankulam and Idinthakarai villages was 9,063 and 3,996 respectively. Site shall be considered as acceptable if implementation of emergency measures under accident conditions can be ensured for the entire population. Offsite emergency response plan prepared should demonstrate adequate capability to handle such situations. A detailed emergency preparedness plan or EPP for an area 16 km around the plant, termed emergency planning zone, which also includes the sterilised zone, is put in place before the start of operation of the plant. This emergency preparedness plan is made available to the district magistrate of the area."

Census figures (2011) for Koodankulam, Vijaypathi and Erukkanduri—all within the 5-km sterilised zone—were pegged at 28,397, higher than the stipulated 20,000, prompting G Sundar Rajan to file a public interest litigation in court related to Units 3-6, located at the same site. The Madras High Court dismissed the PIL saying that several checks and balances had been incorporated in the clearance.

The offsite emergency preparedness plan made by NPCIL according to the statutory guidelines of the National Disaster Management Authority (NDMA) and meant to be implemented along with the district administration, basically applies only to people living in the 16-km emergency planning zone.

(It is worth noting that the Japanese authorities evacuated people from places up to 40 km northwest of the Fukushima plant. All of the land within 20 km of the destroyed nuclear power plant, encompassing an area of 600 sq km, was declared too radioactive for human habitation and the region dubbed a permanent exclusion zone. An estimated 3 lakh Fukushima evacuees are still struggling to cope two years later).

Trans-district, trans-state or trans-national effects of an accident, meanwhile, have not even been considered, according to a section of an affidavit dealing with offsite disaster management by NPCIL filed by G Sundar Rajan in the Supreme Court. All the points where evacuated people can be temporarily accommodated in the event of a disaster are also within distances where there is a very real potential for serious exposure and contamination in the event of a Level 7 accident, the highest level according to the

INES or International Nuclear and Radiological Events Scale (a Level 7 accident at the Koodankulam plant has been ruled out by NPCIL).

Specific emergency shelters to be used (in an offsite emergency) by an estimated 2 lakh population within the 16 km emergency zone (figures according to a fact-finding team of PUCL Tamil Nadu) have not been identified. All of the rallying points for evacuated populations mentioned in the NDMA emergency guidelines are either government or private schools, listed as being able to accommodate between 15,000-35,000 people, a gross over-estimate, according to the petition filed by G Sundar Rajan in the Supreme Court, which also highlights problems of overcrowding, hygiene and sanitation. Periodic training to medical staff at primary health centres in the Tirunelveli area to enable them to function as screening centres, adequate equipment and supplies to deal with patients exposed to radiation, as well as transportation vehicles equipped with first aid to take serious patients to referral hospitals are all mandated in the emergency plan but exist only on paper, Sundar's petition claims.

A multi-specialty hospital, supplies and medical infrastructure capable of dealing with the fall-out of nuclear disasters are all listed requirements that have yet to be fully complied with. The nearest large hospitals are in Kanyakumari and Nagercoil, at least 30 km away from the Koodankulam plant. By NPCIL's own admission (R S Sundar's interview to Rediffmail. com), the plant's hospital has 'two doctors and a few staff'. A hospital in Nagercoil, 30 km away, is contracted to provide medical services round the clock and there is a referral facility available with Apollo Hospital in Chennai, 700 km away. As for the requirement for a super-specialty hospital, there is no network of hospitals anywhere in the country that can handle radiation-induced injuries on a large scale (source: Supreme Court's May 2013 reply to G Sundar Rajan's petition)!

The 'Health Care' column of the 21-page 'Facts on the Koodankulam Nuclear Power Project' report posted on NPCIL's own website mentions only that "several medical camps have been organised in the surrounding villages, hepatitis B vaccinations have been administered to school/village children and hearing aids distributed to schools for the hearing impaired as well".

The National Disaster Management Authority, headed by the prime minister, also decrees periodic training courses for on-site and off-site administrative personnel, including state government officials and various other stakeholders. The police, fire and emergency services, medicos, paramedics, non-governmental organisations, civil defence and home guards have to be fully integrated into nuclear emergency programmes both at the state and district levels. Most of the responsibility for disaster management lies with the district administration and the state government; both have often displayed hostility towards project-affected people, filing 380 cases against more than 227,000 villagers in Idinthakarai and Koodankulam over the past years. The villagers—undeniably the main stakeholders—deny witnessing or participating in any kind of engagement or training or emergency drill undertaken by NPCIL,in the plant's existence.

NPCIL's *Expert Group Report on the Safety of KKNPP* (December 2011), however, reiterates that all plant employees, CISF personnel and 600 officials from government departments like social welfare, fire, electricity, health, police and others have been trained. Plant emergency exercises are mandated once in three months, site emergency exercises once a year and offsite emergency exercises once in two years. The NPCIL website details records of an emergency offsite exercise conducted along with district authorities in June 2012 in a village called Nakkaneri, 7 km from the plant. A few days later, an 8-member Tamil Nadu PUCL team conducted a fact-finding investigation at Nakkaneri, recommending that the Offsite Emergency Preparedness Exercise "reportedly" conducted on June 9, 2012 in Nakkaneri be declared "null and void", as it was a "mockery on all national and international regulatory codes". Their findings were based on testimonies given by Nakkaneri villagers that no "nuclear emergency training" had been given to them during the exercise with respect to either evacuation or disaster management drill. Moreover most of the villagers were out at work, only children and the elderly were present during the exercise.

In a similar experience, everyone I spoke to in the various villages I visited denied knowledge of any disaster or emergency preparedness exercises or training, or even awareness about their existence.

In a nutshell therefore, it is reasonable to assume that if you live less than a kilometre away from a nuclear plant that you are opposing and if it begins operations regardless of your 678-day protests and if there is an accident at the said plant, this would be your probable course of action: you do not know what to do at the first sign of trouble except panic since you have not been warned except for a newspaper article telling you to cover your mouth and shut your doors and windows. You do not know where and how you will be evacuated; if it is to a school within a 30-km radius, you will be equally affected there. You will also share your troubles—and drinking water and perhaps a total of five bathrooms—with at least 15,000 fellow evacuees. If you are injured you will make your way to a PHC that may or may not have the medicines and trained doctors to treat your radiation-specific symptoms; the transportation vans, organised by an administration that has been unresponsive, even hostile to you in the past, may or may not have a fully equipped first aid kit to take you over fairly uncomfortable roads to a super-specialty hospital because there isn't one in the vicinity.

And if you don't survive all this, your family will receive no insurance because the nuclear liability and insurance laws do not compensate victims of a nuclear disaster. The General Insurance Corporation (GIC) has not provided insurance to any nuclear reactor in the country under the Civil Liability Nuclear Damage Act; this Act enables the operator of nuclear power plants in India (NPCIL) to seek only partial compensation from suppliers in case of accidents. Individual victims cannot sue anyone; only the operator—NPCIL—can sue the manufacturers or suppliers within a limited period of 10 years. The maximum amount payable by foreign companies is capped at Rs 1,500 crore as provided under the Nuclear Liability Act passed in 2010 by both houses of parliament. The actual risk liability for the Koodankulam plant could be several times that amount, experts estimate.

The Russian reactor manufacturing company has refused to share any part of civil liability in case of an accident due to a defect in their own reactor, citing an Indo-Russian inter-governmental secret agreement signed in 2008 absolving them (the suppliers) of any liability at all. The public exchequer or tax payers will have to pay up in case the Russian reactors are not 'a hundred percent safe' as they are claimed to be, while the Russians themselves are indemnified. The text of the 2008 secret agreement between the two countries has never been made public.

The Russian company that refused to share any liability was Atomstroyexport, a subsidiary of the Russian State Atomic Energy Corporation, Rosatom. In February 2012, Zio-Podolsk's procurement director Sergei Shutov was arrested by the Federal Security Service or FSB (successor to the KGB) for buying low quality raw materials at cheaper rates and pocketing the difference. Zio-Podolsk delivered steam generators for nuclear plants for Rosatom's clients in China, Iran, Bulgaria and India.

PMANE's Uday Kumar narrates the unmasking of the Zio-Podolsk-Koodankulam-NPCIL connection, the story taking on a faintly whodunit flavour! He begins: "We are fighting at two levels—popular mobilisation and the intellectual level. At the second level, we collect information from RTI, dig out information from the internet, collate it, ask questions. At the end of 2012, we stumbled upon the information that Zio-Podolsk's Sergei Shutov was arrested in February 2012, so we started asking if there was any equipment received at the Koodankulam plant from that company. Since we knew one person working in the project, we asked him if he had seen any equipment with the Zio-Podolsk name-tag on it. We also asked AERB an RTI question: 'Has AERB received any equipment from this company, since their person has been arrested, and we want to check out the quality issue'.

"NPCIL's one-sentence answer was totally different to our question. They said: 'No information on such inquiries is available with us'. Our internet research showed that A P Joshi, special secretary in the DAE, went to Russia in July 2012, four months after Shutov's arrest. We found out that the A P Joshi team actually visited Zio-Podolsk. So we asked AERB (through another RTI application):'If you don't know anything about this, how is it that A P Joshi went to Zio-Podolsk and you still claim that you don't know anything about it?' Then they were caught and said: 'We *have* received some components from this company.' This was a complete chance discovery. One has to be on the internet, look up the Russian sites and translate all of it.

"Similarly, we found out that Alexander Murach, the head of Informtekh, another Russian supplier company, was arrested and imprisoned for three years in Russia. We asked them the same thing and they showed complete innocence. When we pointed out that the A P Joshi team visited all these places in Russia they found they couldn't hide and said 'yes'. So this is how we manage to get information. Then V Narayansamy (MOS in the PMO) started talking about four valves being faulty and we found that those valves came from Zio-Podolsk," ends Uday.

No independent verification has been conducted on the quality of the components supplied by Zio-Podolsk till date. The NPCIL response at the time was: "During testing of thousands of valves installed in the plant, the performance of four valves of a particular type was found deficient. As corrective measures, the valve components are being replaced by NPCIL and their performance is further being subjected to regulatory review."

The overall culture of corruption and inefficiency has crippled the Koodankulam plant, says Uday. Nuclear officials, politicians and bureaucrats have compromised the safety of the people by buying untested, unproved technology and sub-standard parts from Russia.

In an article posted online (in *Dianuke*), Dr A Gopalakrishnan, nuclear scientist and former AERB chairman, points out: "After the signing of the Indo-Russia agreement in 1988, the USSR disintegrated in 1991; the subsidiary units which were supplying components for the Russian nuclear establishment also fell into undesirable hands. The arrest of the Zio-Podolsk executive in connection with the distribution of cheap and fraudulent materials to reactors is shocking because the same company had supplied components to the nuclear reactor at Koodankulam. Let the Russian authorities themselves come here, examine the entire components and certify that they are of good quality," Gopalakrishnan writes.

Dr Ramesh Radhakrishnan, PMANE technical team expert, describes their initial interest in theKoodankulam reactor which later changed to dismay and disillusionment. "Koodankulam is the biggest machine Indian technical people have ever handled; there is no turbine above this height in India. It was the first experience in more than 50 years of India's technical literacy-- being able to handle a machine imported from Russia, with the language gap. We also thought initially that the machine was wonderful. Till January 2013, we even felt it would start despite the protests but time and again they (NPCIL) were unable to start the machine. We were also curious about the reason, so then we investigated the history of how this machine was made; we discovered literature written in Russian, Chinese and Czech languages, got it translated and shared it with the people operating the plant as well," says Dr Ramesh with a flourish.

The information that Dr Ramesh, Dr Pugazhendhi and Dr V T Padmanabhan uncovered and pieced together was essentially that "old, rusting, unused, broken-down equipment lying in dump-yards for 10-15 years, after the cancellation of production of all nuclear reactors for the period 1990-96, post-Chernobyl," was palmed off to countries like China, India and Iran. "It was counterfeit, sub-standard equipment that was sent here to

Koodankulam," declares Dr Ramesh.

The same PMANE technical team also published a book *Koodankulam Atomic Reactor: Unscientific Methods* (written in Tamil) as source material for the campaign against KKNPP and to "anchor scientific credentials for why the site was not suitable for a nuclear power plant"; the team also provided studies to show that a near-field tsunami *was* possible at the site (caused by shifting sands 60 km away in the south Gulf of Munnar) and that the coast shoreline was not stable as claimed by the authorities. "We pushed the scientific narrative, we studied manuals that talk about how to make yourself ready for a tsunami, how to plan a nuclear reactor against a tsunami so as to ensure safety," says Dr Ramesh.

Perhaps one of the most significant problems related to people's safety—yet to be addressed and shared with the public, especially those it will affect directly—is what will be done with the highly radioactive and very toxic nuclear waste (spent fuel) once the plant begins commercial operations. Under the 1988 agreement between India and Russia, radioactive waste was to be transported back to Russia. This was reversed in the 1998 agreement where NPCIL declared that it would be stored at the KKNPP site for at least 10 years. Handling and storage of this waste involves high risks and serious environmental implications. NPCIL and AERB have not, as yet, earmarked a place for permanent burial and storage, other than mentioning that spent fuel will be kept in storage pools at the site.

According to Sekhar Basu, chief executive of the Nuclear Recycle Board, reprocessing would need several permissions and many procedures though the technology for doing so was available in India. An integrated nuclear recycle plant would come up by 2020. "Since we generate power there will be some waste. And this waste is only two to three per cent of the total fuel we put into the reactor. Entire spent fuel is not waste; plutonium and uranium are recycled which contribute to about 97-98 per cent of the spent fuel. So only the remaining two to three per cent of spent fuel is waste. This waste can be divided into two parts - one where within 300 years, 99 per cent of the waste becomes non-radioactive and the rest (which)is going to remain radioactive for a longer time. So we are working towards the development of a process where we can separate waste that becomes non-radioactive within 300 years," declared Sekhar Basu in media interactions in 2012.

Uday refutes these figures: "The waste will be radioactive for 48,000 years; the half-life will be 24,000 years. DAE officials had spoken of a reprocessing plant in Koodankulam earlier." The Supreme Court May 6, 2013 judgement caps the half-life of spent fuel at 1,70,000 years.

If the site meant to store 99% of nuclear waste that will remain radioactive for 300 years—taking the most conservative figure—is yet to be identified for a reactor regularly predicted to begin commercial operations soon, is this not reason enough to validate the fears of those living there today? The NPCIL expert group report clarifies that at KKNPP, spent fuel from the reactors "will be carefully stored in storage pools" that are high-integrity concrete pools with additional stainless steel sheet lining. The spent fuel will be transported "through both railways and by roadways" to an as-yet-unspecified reprocessing facility "in a safe manner without any public hazard".

G Sundar Rajan of Friends of Earth and member of the PMANE legal/environment expert group explains: "All international nuclear plants including Koodankulam will be under international safeguards so you cannot take uranium (spent fuel) to a place which does not have the safeguard. India has three reprocessing plants—one small one in Trombay only for a test reactor, Tarapur and Kalpakkam—but they are not under international safeguards, so waste from Koodankulam cannot be taken to either.So where will it be taken? We have received no answer," he shrugs.

Uday underscores these doubts: "Even the Supreme Court failed to raise this question. If the Koodankulam waste is not going to be buried in Kolar (in the disused mines of the Kolar Gold Fields) then where else will it? 'We will cross that bridge when we come to it' cannot be the answer to this important issue. They want to build a nuclear Taj Mahal without any toilet!"

According to PMANE reports, even the very hot, mildly radioactive coolant water from the reactor that will be off-loaded into the sea at 7 degrees Centigrade is likely to severely impact fish catch, undermining the fishing industry and livelihood of fisher-folk in the region.

When environmental clearance was first issued in 1989, cooling water for the project was to be drawn from the Pechiparai reservoir. The source was later changed to four desalination plants drawing water from the sea. This substantial change in freshwater source necessitated a fresh EC, as also clearances under the Coastal Regulation Zone (CRZ), which PMANE leaders allege have not been obtained. The Supreme Court May 6, 2013 order dismissed the need for a fresh CRZ clearance.

In an interview to NDTV in September 2012, after the confrontation between protestors and the police, Environment Minister Jayanti Natarajan said: "The plant is absolutely safe, is fully compliant with environmental norms; the 7 degree Centigrade water release as prescribed in the EC (the later EC of September 2008) will not harm fish, marine life or people living around the plant. A new EIA is not necessary at this point."

In sharp contradiction, anti-nuke groups point out that even when KKNPP functions normally, without any incidents and accidents, it would be emitting iodine 131, 132, 133, cesium-134, 136, 137 isotopes, strontium, tritium, tellurium and other such radioactive particles into the air, land, crops, cattle, sea, seafood and groundwater, thereby adding to existing health concerns in the southern coastal belt.

NPCIL (source: *Expert Group Report on Safety of KKNPP*) repudiates any link between the incidence of cancer and genetic effects of exposure to low-level radiation with the following explanation:

> *The levels of radiation from nuclear plants don't exceed a small fraction of even the variation in natural radiation back-ground. In fact the philosophy of the International Commission on Radiological Protection (ICRP) in setting limits of exposure to the public is inter alia to consider the variation in dose from natural radiation to which the public is always subjected. Some areas have natural background radiation which is much higher due to radiation-emitting thorium/uranium-bearing minerals. The western coast of Kerala and some coastal areas of Tamil Nadu receive five times more radiation dose than elsewhere. The public around Koodankulam will not receive more than 1% of this dose due to the operation of KKNPP, so there will be no deleterious effects due to radiation.*

According to AERB stipulations in 1989, radioactive release should be maintained in line with ALARA (As Low As Reasonably

Achievable) values of radiation exposure to occupational workers and members of the public.

Dr Pugazhendhi, also known as Dr Pugal, is a medical practitioner based in Kalpakkam who has conducted studies and surveys for over a decade on the effects of radiation on the health of people living near the Kalpakkam nuclear plant. His studies have been published in various media outlets and have been shared with the health division of the Kalpakkam plant, which he claims has not denied his findings. "They (Kalpakkam plant officials) only say radiation from the plant is too low to cause any health effects, which is scientifically incorrect as there is no safe dosage in low-level radiation. International agencies such as the International Commission on Radiological Protection (ICRP) and the International Renewable Energy Agency (IREA) concur. X-rays, gamma rays, neutrons were declared carcinogens officially in January 2005; the European Union banned the use of X-rays at airports in November 2011, switching to safer alternatives. Doesn't that show that there is no safe dose of radiation? What kind of legacy are we leaving for society," asks Dr Pugal passionately.

He claims that according to United Nations data (*UNSCEAR 2000 Report*, Volume 1), radiation from Indian nuclear power plants is far higher than that from those in Western countries. Dr Pugal cites the Energy Employees Occupational Illness Compensation Programme Act of October 2000 (in use in countries like Japan and the US) to illustrate the link between radiation-induced illness and nuclear power plants in a normal, non-accident scenario. There is no comparable legislation in India nor has any all-India study been published by government to examine the cause and effect of radiation from nuclear power plants on the health and wellbeing of those who live near them. Specific individual studies, organisational studies (commissioned by the DAE) and media reports based on RTI queries have estimated this impact in different nuclear plants over different states—a difficult task as cancers can have a variety of causal agents.

Dr Pugal's own studies include polydactyl cases in children—children born with extra fingers or toes—and deaths due to multiple myeloma in 2003, thyroid anomalies in 2007 and auto-immune thyroid diseases in 2008 and 2010. In the polydactyl survey, he documented evidence of 12 cases of polydactyl in children living within the 16-km radius of the Kalpakkam Atomic Power Station (KAPS); all the children were born after KAPS was set up. The AERB denied any link between radiation release and polydactyl.

In the case of multiple myeloma or bone cancer as a result of radiation, Dr Pugal found that among employees and wards of the Kalpakkam plant, three persons had died due to this disease over a period of 18 months. The BARC's official response was that the amount of radiation they had all received was well within AERB limits.

"How do you determine whether radiation causes a disease?" asks Dr Pugal. "It (statistics of the disease) should be more near the nuclear plant, and if you go away it should be less. Even in the vicinity of the plant it should be more, to be statistically significant, which is what I had shown in my studies, first with multiple myeloma in 2003 and then with auto immune thyroid diseases (AITD) among fisherfolk women living near the plant, as a result of radiation exposure. The data was accepted by the DAE but their reply was that the amount of radiation coming out of the plant was too small to cause any thyroidism," says Dr Pugal. He also mentions that as per the raw data in studies conducted by DAE-appointed epidemiologist Dr Manjula Datta, the figure for mental retardation was 11 times higher, cancer seven times higher and thyroid problems five times higher in villages near the Kalpakkam plant.

"The government promises that there will be no health-related problems with the Koodankulam plant, but in any plant there is liquid, solid and gaseous waste," says Dr Pugal, "and my studies on multiple myeloma and thyroid cancer have not been contested on the grounds of scientific evidence or statistical significance. All the DAE can say in the case of my Kalpakkam study is that other carcinogens could have caused the cancers and that it is comparable to the national average. But there is no scientific study conducted by the DAE to prove that other carcinogens caused the cancers, so how can you say it is *not* caused by radiation from the plant?" he argues.

In their paper, 'The Price We Pay' (published in *Prisoners of the Nuclear Dream*), noted physicist Surendra Gadekar and M V Ramana detail the "only power station in India around which there has been a scientific study of health consequences on the local population, not just the workers in the plant—Rajasthan Atomic Power Station, located at Rawatbhata near Kota in central India". This study conducted in 1991 surveyed five villages (total population: 2,860) within 10 km of the plant and compared them with four other villages (total population: 2,544) more than 50 km away. The results were published in 1993. The study observed an increase in the rate of congenital deformities, a significantly higher rate of spontaneous abortions, stillbirths and one-day deaths of newborn babies, a significant increase in chronic diseases especially among the young, a significant increase in solid tumours, and more cancer patients and cancer deaths in villages near the plant.

In Kerala, Dr V T Padmanabhan conducted a cohort (group) study from 1988-1994, of the correlation between radiation and genetic disorders in a population of 38,000 people living on a 26-km island—Chavara, Neendakara, Alapat and Panmana villages—that receives higher radiation from the monazite sand on its beaches. The control group of 32,000 people—the ones not exposed to the radiation—lived in three villages of Alapuzha district and were similar in all other criteria such as caste, occupation, lifestyle.

The results of the study, published in the *International Journal of Health Services*, showed that children on the island with background radiation had a three times higher chance of having Down's Syndrome; there was a 50% increase in all proven genetic disorders. There was also a higher incidence of untoward pregnancy outcomes such as miscarriages or infant and child deaths when both parents were from the same village.

The documentary film, *Buddha Weeps in Jadugoda*, by Shriprakash highlights the devastating effects of uranium mining in Jadugoda where radioactive waste has been dumped into the rice fields of adivasis for the last 30 years. The film documents the link between slow deaths and genetic mutations and excessive radiation as a result of unsafe uranium mining.

The Times of India published a front-page article in 2014 linking cancer-related deaths to atomic energy establishments across the country over 20 years, based on an RTI reply given to activist Chetan Kothari. "Cancer caused almost 70% of the 3,887 deaths caused by ailments in the atomic energy hubs across the country over 20 years... 2,600 succumbed to cancer in 19 centres between 1995 and 2014. Most of the deceased in the report were between 29-50 years old."The data revealed in the query to the Bhabha Atomic Research Centre (BARC) which is under the DAE, like the other nuclear establishments, also mentioned 225 suicides in the same period, roughly one every month for 20 years, on account of prolonged illness or family problems.

Dr Altaf Patel, a senior physician quoted in the article, stated that such high cancer mortality was alarming and needed to be analysed to check if it occurred among people who were in touch with radioactive material. Dr Shashank Joshi, president of the Association of Physicians of India, while agreeing that there is an established link between cancer and radiation, stated that he was a bit sceptical about the data as it was difficult to establish the cause and effect correlation without studying the cases. He added that if the BARC data showed such high cancer mortality there was a need for stringent safety standards.

In response to a further RTI query filed by the same activist asking for details of major and minor accidents that have happened at India's nuclear plants, NPCIL's reply was that no accident had ever taken place, a claim slammed by scientists, filmmakers and anti-nuke activists, with Greenpeace citing at least 20 accidents over the last two decades.

According to the US Environment Protection Agency, the amount and duration of radiation exposure affects the severity or type of health effects: stochastic effects that are associated with long-term, low-level (chronic) exposure to radiation (cancer, changes in DNA, genetic mutations passed on to offspring) and non-stochastic effects associated with short-term, high-level or 'acute' exposure to radiation. In stochastic effects, even though each radionuclide represents a somewhat different health risk, health physicists currently estimate that, overall, if each person in a group of 10,000 people is exposed to 1 rem (unit of radiation dose) of ionizing radiation in small doses over a lifetime, five or six more people would die of cancer than otherwise (in the usual rate of exposure, most people receive about 3/10ths of rem each year from natural background sources of radiation).

Children are more sensitive to radiation than adults, so are foetuses. The National Academy of Sciences maintains that no dose of radiation is safe; every dose increases the danger of cancer or genetic disease. It declares that children are 10-20 times more vulnerable to radiation's carcinogenic effects, and foetuses 1,000 times more sensitive.

Teratogenic mutations result from the exposure of foetuses to radiation and can include smaller head or brain size, poorly formed eyes, abnormally slow growth and mental retardation; foetuses are most sensitive between 8-15 weeks after conception— four out of 1,000 would be born mentally retarded if exposed to 1 rem. Genetic effects passed from parent to child are estimated by health experts as follows: approximately 50 severe hereditary effects would occur in a group of 1 million live-born children whose parents were both exposed to 1 rem. About 120 severe hereditary effects would occur in all descendants. Unlike cancer, non-stochastic health effects (burns and radiation sickness) appear quickly and if the dose is fatal, death usually occurs within two months.

"Women are the first to get affected by radiation since it affects the ovaries. No woman wants a deformed child. We saw how people got destroyed in the Fukushima tragedy; we protest so that our people can live and don't face the same fate," Milret said to me in an interview in Idinthakarai. When Milret of Idinthakarai or Rani of Tsunami Colony or Parthimma of

Koodankulam speak about anxieties related to their families—of thyroid cancer, of deformed babies/children, of a shortened lifespan—they are not imagining monsters that don't exist.

NPCIL terms this "fear of genetic effects of radiation around nuclear sites more psychological and contrary to scientific facts...a fear/concern which is due to a lack of understanding and awareness in the public mind about radiation and its effects on health. In order to remove such misgivings, authorities of nuclear power sites carry out awareness programmes...People are invited and taken on guided tours, officials visit villages...Once people are sensitised it will help remove misconceptions and they will treat a nuclear emergency like any other natural or man-made emergency".

Clearly, the 'authorities' of *this* particular nuclear site will have to work a lot harder to reach, convince and sensitise the project-affected people. For now, they are sitting firmly on the other side of the Koodankulam fence.

I recall asking the fiery Xavier Amma the very first time I met her that if the government had already spent Rs 13,171 crore on the plant till date, how would they abandon it? Her reply was immediate and astonishing: "That amount is not much for them. One woman, Kanimozhi, swindled (the government) out of Rs 170,000 crore, stayed in jail for a short time and is free now. What did they do to her? We can pay Rs 13,000 crore, but ask that the plant be halted."

The Koodankulam project's initial cost at the time of signing the agreement in 1988 was Rs 6,000 crore. This increased to Rs 13,171 crore for Unit 1 to be completed by December 2007 and Unit 2 by December 2008 (NPCIL figures). Russia advanced a credit amount of Rs 6,416 crore. MOS V Narayansamy disclosed that the project cost of Units 1 and 2 have increased by 14% due to delays, to reach Rs 15,454 crore by January 2013. The sanctioned cost now stands revised at Rs 17,270 crore with further revisions coming up. PMANE's Uday Kumar reveals that in an RTI reply dated February 20, 2013, the NPCIL authorities claim that the Rs 4,000 crore cost overrun is due to the "increase in interest during construction (IDC), escalation on works, contractors' overheads and establishment charges". The Russian government is not going to compensate India financially for this delay and cost overrun, points out Uday pertinently.

The estimated cost of Units 3 and 4 is projected at Rs 39,747 crore largely on account of uncertainty between Russia and India over the nuclear liability law.

These costs exclude other elements of nuclear power that are difficult to quantify, such as the long-term cost of waste processing and management, cost of decommissioning (closing down and dismantling a nuclear plant safely) which is again not measurable in the absence of actual experience of foolproof decommissioning of any plant in the world. Experts estimate that in the case of Fukushima, closing down and dismantling the Dai-ichi plant will take from an optimistic 40 years to an unknown "thousands of years" and cost between 330-420 billion dollars. The extreme variation in estimates is because of lack of a credible decommissioning technology and science in the world, even today.

The pay-off of these rising costs for Tamil Nadu is an estimated 925 MW or roughly 50% of the power generated from KKNPP, while neighbouring states receive 35%—442 MW for Karnataka, 266 MW for Kerala, 67 MW for Puducherry and the remaining 15% unallocated power added to the central pool.

NPCIL promises that the Koodankulam plant—expected

to have a production life of 60 years, extendable for another 20 years—is slated to provide electricity at an 'affordable' rate of Rs 2.50 per unit, as against the Rs 3.50 per unit charged in Tamil Nadu. This constitutes the last component of NPCIL's premise of nuclear energy being the "cleaner, safer and *cheaper* option"; all they have to do now is get the villagers living near the plant to believe it. Along with the grandiose projections made by Prime Minister Manmohan Singh in 2009 that India would have 470 GW of nuclear energy by 2050, more than a hundred times the capacity that existed at that time.

In M V Ramana's book *Power of Promise: Examining Nuclear Energy in India* there is an interesting quote (chapter 1) that perhaps best encapsulates the many promises and projections made with respect to India's nuclear power:

> *The continued expectation that nuclear power will, some day, energise the country in a substantial fashion is well captured by what Fitzgerald says about the eponymous hero of the book, The Great Gatsby:*

> "*Gatsby believed in the green light, the orgiastic future that year by year recedes before us. It eluded us then, but that's no matter—tomorrow we will run faster, stretch out our arms farther... And one fine morning—*

> *So we beat on, boats against the current, borne back ceaselessly into the past.*"

Chapter Six

LIFE AFTER THE PLANT GOES 'CRITICAL'

At 11.05 pm on July 13, 2013, Unit 1 of the 1,000 MW Koodankulam nuclear power plant attained criticality—a state in which a nuclear fission reaction becomes self-sustaining, a state crucial for generating electricity in a reactor—finally providing a landmark moment for its operator NPCIL.

January 4, 2014

'Aha Aha Anushakti! Aha Aha Anushakti!' (How wonderful is nuclear energy!), a robust male voice sings cheerfully to the accompaniment of loud background music till the phone is finally answered. This is the caller tune of R S Sundar, site director of the Koodankulam power project, and this is my first call to ask for an interview with him in Koodankulam, preferably in the plant premises. An introductory email providing details and my credentials has already been sent earlier from Mumbai. He listens to my request and says he is busy for the next two days. I ask for time on any of the subsequent six days, which throws him momentarily but he promises to revert soon.

Meanwhile Idinthakarai wears an almost festive look on this

873rd day of the women's relay protest, flagging off the national convention of anti-nuke groups slated to begin in an hour. Village loudspeakers belt out Tamil songs at 9.30 am, women bustle around carrying large utensils, men with plastic chairs walk briskly towards a community hall in the distance. "Mildred *amma, yenakkaga kathirungal!*" (Wait for me!) says Bhargavi, a young Delhi-based activist working for Programme for Social Action. A joyous reunion follows with lots of hugging and excited chatter in Tamil.

Bhargavi considers Idinthakarai home, having rebelled against her "middle class, luxurious Brahmin family home" and the "cosy AC cabin" in the IT company she worked for earlier, in the days when environmental protection, for the middle class, only meant hugging trees. The women of Idinthakarai are among her biggest role models today. She accompanies them to the hall where they set up their kitchen in the adjoining alcove and then checks the main hall in preparation for the two-day national convention of anti-nuclear movements that will kickstart PMANE's campaign for 2014.

As participants (activists from across the country) settle down in an informal circle in the spacious, airy hall, Ryan welcomes them, saying: "This is *your* village, *your* struggle." Uday then outlines the agenda for the sessions that are grouped under the title 'Confronting the Nuke-Colonisation of India'. The discussion that unfolds--in an orderly, democratic fashion with each speaker adhering to the allotted time before Question Hour—is a remarkably forthright self-appraisal of anti-nuke movements in India: its shortfalls and possible solutions.

Given the pan-national theme of the convention, the debates are in English, so the residents of Idinthakarai or Tsunami Colony or Koodankulam and nearby villages that are part of the struggle are unable to participate. But I do catch glimpses of familiar faces helping serve tea, preparing lunch and welcoming 'outsiders' to the venue. And of course they occupy centrestage for the entire duration of the convention as speaker after speaker raises his/her voice on their behalf.

"The Prime Minister has taken us back to colonial times, only this time it is nuke-colonisation, aggressively expanding nuclear power generation and enhancing nuclear business with the help of nuclear powers such as the United States, Russia, France and others," says Uday in his introductory statement. "Both the Congress and BJP are complicit in this colonisation. Nuclear energy is projected as our salvation, a single solution for India's lack of energy security, military security and overall national security. We are problematising the issue of nuclear colonisation of India; how do we step in, who are the new *bhadralok* who will help? We need to raise our voice now, however feeble, however remote. It needs to be heard. We need to take it out of Idinthakarai, to the rest of India. Let us think collectively about how to confront this issue and come up with a set of resolutions."

In the two days that follow, crammed with hours of impassioned dialogue, free-flowing exchange of ideas, often unflattering self-analysis, arguments across lunch tables and informal group sessions divided geographically according to state-wise representation, several possibilities for action emerge. Lalita Ramdas, the vivacious and outspoken anti-nuke activist and founder of Greenpeace India, minces no words while pointing out that the Koodankulam struggle has to be made a mass movement. "We need to be sharper, clearer on nuclear policy; the Koodankulam struggle has shown amazing sustainability but irrespective of how many people sign our charter of demands, who will look at it? Even in terms of the decision-makers, will they respond? It's not catching the popular imagination, people are not signed on in an intelligent way, nowhere else are we able to convince people that there is actually a danger. The PMANE leadership has done a great job even though it is confined to this area, but where do we go to convince people? We need an alternative to do that, we need a clear political option, it cannot be done by a movement alone," she urges earnestly.

Lalita Ramdas and her husband Admiral Ramdas (retired chief of naval staff and also an avowed anti-nuke activist) have recently joined the Aam Aadmi Party and are wearing AAP badges to the convention. There are rumours that PMANE leaders, especially Uday Kumar, may contest the 2014 general elections as AAP candidates, and work towards incorporating the anti-nuke agenda into its national agenda.

For the present however, Uday declares that PMANE is not part of any political party; it is beyond party politics. There is a need to educate leaders and continue to write to different political parties. "Six months ago, we wrote letters to all the political parties but we received not a single reply," Uday says regretfully. A myriad alternatives (to the political option) follow in quick succession and in no particular order.

"Passion and framing are both important in sending out your message," says the articulate and colourfully-clad environmental journalist Nityanand Jayaraman. You need to approach the issue differently, he advises. For example, one can contrast the 14-hour power cuts in Tamil Nadu with Mukesh Ambani's electricity bill of Rs 76 lakh a month for his 75-storey home, to illustrate inequity. "The anti-nuke movement did have successful moments after Fukushima, for example. The frame (of an issue) at that time was 'nuclear power is dangerous'; after some time, it faded. 'Activism equals Maoism equals foreign funding' became powerful frames that worked very well with people believing them," analyses Nityanand.

He suggests targeting inefficiency in the power sector—eliminating transmission and distribution losses, reducing wasteful use of electricity such as the lighting of malls and billboards 24/7, and several efficiency enhancement measures. Reach out and talk to the younger generation—even schoolchildren—especially in the urban sector, involve them in campaigns, he adds (the Chennai Solidarity Group did in fact launch campaigns such as 'Leaky Bucket', pointing out losses and wastage in the electricity sector and highlighting efficiency enhancement measures).

Who is the audience, how do you reach it, and what is the long-term impact of creating awareness about nuclear power, asks Nityanand. This is the key concern voiced by most activists participating inside this medium-sized room in a small village, 700 km from the state capital Chennai which, in turn, is 2,172 km from the policymakers and decision-takers in New Delhi. Why do anti-nuke movements make only sporadic impact? Why are they unable to change policy at the power centres? Why is the anti-nuke argument not too popular with audiences, especially urban consumers? After detailed, interactive soul-searching, the solutions seem to point to emphasising renewable energy options—solar, wind, geo-thermal, biofuel, bio-energy, biogas, tidal energy.

Let's not be anti-nuclear activists, let's be safe energy activists, suggests G Sundar Rajan of Friends of Earth, the environmental NGO that is also a key component of PMANE's expert team. Bhargavi calls it being pro-earth instead of anti-nuclear or anti-coal or anti-hydro, anti-big dams. "This movement has been the biggest inspiration in my life; for the last two years I've been helping with specific interest groups such as Artists for Koodankulam or Writers for Koodankulam," says Bhargavi. "I've seen that small things have a big impact. But whenever I would meet MPs in Delhi as part of my campaign work, they wouldn't care to even listen let alone understand the nuclear issue. Perhaps they would listen to a pro-safe energy one," she says. Uday chimes in smilingly: "We are warriors of the earth. Let's call ourselves Mother Earth's Army!"

This is the more acceptable face of the movement around which successful strategies can be built: highlighting for example the sustained school campaigns for safe energy in West Bengal and the inroads made in Kerala, says Shantanu Chakravarty from Kolkata, emphasising the continued use of Facebook, Twitter and all forms of social media in state-wide campaigns.

"We have a 25-year familiarity with the nuclear issue in Kerala so we can share our experiences with others. The people's movement managed to halt two nuclear power stations—Peringome and Kothamangalam—so there is a need to connect with other anti-nuke movements," says Kerala-based N Subramaniam. Since this is in fact the main goal of the convention, everyone agrees to build on each other's ideas to create what Lalita Ramdas called "a concrete plan of action".

Recommendations for the wish-list that needs to be turned into reality follow quickly: a white paper on alternative energy sources; a paper pointing out the dangers of nuclear power; coordination in the struggles against upcoming plants in Jaitapur, Haripur, Kovvada, Fatehabad, Mithi Virdi and others; countering government's stand on health and safety of nuclear power plants with information provided by our own technical experts and scientists; disseminating and highlighting flaws in nuclear plants to larger audiences; documenting and sharing lessons learnt from the Koodankulam struggle so that their voices can be heard by government.

The official part of the convention concludes with Uday releasing a formal resolution denouncing the Indo-US nuclear deal and expressing solidarity with all struggles resisting nuclear projects in various parts of India (Fatehabad, Haripur, Jaitapur, Kovvada, Mithi Virdi, Banswada, Chutka, Koodankulam, Kalpakkam, Thevaram, Madurai, Manavalakurichi, Pazhayakayal and Jadugoda).

At the Samara *pandal*, as part of the closing ceremony, Tamil political leaders hold forth with fiery oratory as the afternoon sun casts shadows on the sandy floor where the women sit, listening attentively while their small children play within touching distance. A toddler seated in his mother's lap, all bundled up in a woollen cap, stares at me solemnly whilst his mother joins in the enthusiastic applause as the speaker's voice reaches an impressive crescendo. The men sit on the edges of the *pandal*, or to one side on coloured plastic chairs, and I wonder again at the divide: shouldn't these women who are leading the movement be treated on a par with the men? Or is this an urban perspective and irrelevant here? The crowd disperses once the VIPs leave with their security convoys.

Amal Raj breaks up an impromptu meeting of PMANE leaders and visiting speakers to announce the evening's entertainment—a screening of the documentary film *Gere Dan* (For the supreme fight) in the Jalonke language of Mali, Western

Africa. The 46-minute film, which is in French with English subtitles, is set in the remote region of Mali where uranium deposits were discovered by French company Areva, the world's largest nuclear company, in a small village named Falea, which had no basic amenities. The film explores the truth behind the uranium mining industry's claims of providing for the poorest of the poor.

The familiar Samara *pandal* is set up with a projector and a roll-down white screen, filmmaker Shriprakash facing his audience comprising the women (and some men) and children of Idinthakarai. For the next 90 minutes, even though the language is alien (Bhargavi translates large chunks of the film by pausing it at regular intervals and providing a précis), the content is not; there is a basic identification with what is happening onscreen.

The children—visibly bored—have by now gone to sleep in their mothers' laps or stretched out on the sandy floor. Their mothers on the other hand—despite the lateness of the hour and the alien language and translation breaks—step up to ask an impressed Shriprakash questions about what Areva is doing to the locals in Africa, displaying what he calls "a remarkable level of political awareness". They also quiz him on updates and comparisons between Koodankulam and Jadugoda, having seen his earlier documentary *Buddha Weeps in Jadugoda* on the hazardous effects of uranium mining on the tribals there. Others in the audience such as Admiral Ramdas and Lalita Ramdas have a few more questions for the intrepid filmmaker before the crowd disperses.

Ryan informs me later that the villagers are accustomed to such film screenings as PMANE tries to hold at least one every two months; this frequent use of the audio-visual medium, as also access to many books in the library cupboard in the church foyer, is one reason for the high level of social awareness on such issues in Idinthakarai.

~

Sonorous hymns pouring out of the many speakers at 5 am herald the morning Mass and ensure an early day for most people, and most certainly for me. I request Amal Raj to help plan visits to the nearby villages of Vijaypati, Perumenal, Koothankuthzi, Koodankulam and Tsunami Colony to find out what people feel now that KKNPP has gone critical. We begin with the nearest, both to Idinthakarai and to the plant—Tsunami Colony. A flashy green 10-seater jeep rattles along the short ride to Tsunami Colony, the garrulous driver offering to wait for us till we complete our round of interviews.

Retracing my earlier route, I approach the row of houses nearest the plant. Rani Kervin's first, once again. This time around she comes out all smiles, offers tea and settles down to chat with me. How has your life changed in the last five to six months since the plant went critical? Her reply is surprising: "We don't believe that the plant has really started. They (NPCIL) are lying that electricity has been produced because then there would have been smoke and sounds but there is nothing. Earlier, during the trial runs, we would hear sounds with a half-hour gap in between and also see white and black smoke; also, when white smoke rises from the plant, the sea water becomes hot up to 1.5 km. That is not happening now," Rani says almost gleefully.

Last year you told me you would continue your struggle to ensure the plant does not start functioning. But now what is your stand? How long can you continue to fight the government,

I ask. Her reply is immediate and self-assured: "We will fight, we have faith in god. Recently we did not have power for four days, but we managed (Tirunelveli and Kanyakumari districts have 100% electricity connections in rural areas). We will not stop protesting till they shut down the plant. When we become old our children will continue our protest." What about NPCIL officials who claim that the plant is producing 400 MW of electricity presently(KKNPP Site director R S Sundar quoted in *The Hindu* in December 2013)? "Well, if they don't say that, how will they get their salary," she asks me with a chuckle.

That seems to be the perfect cue to call R S Sundar again to remind him about the interview. I listen to an uninterrupted *Aha Aha Anushakti* caller tune before the line is disconnected.

I walk on towards Tamilarasi's home; her oldest daughter Luvsana—of collector-confronting fame—greets me first, inside the small living room where she is studying. I ask her smilingly if she has met the collector again and she informs me that she is now studying for her exams and collectors can wait! She sets aside her books for 10 minutes to answer my questions, speaking almost before Amal Raj can complete his translation. We don't believe the plant is producing any 'current' so why bother talking about it, she says scornfully. When the trial run was on we could hear so much noise but now when NPCIL says power is being produced we cannot hear a sound. As students we will continue to spread awareness about the plant and its harmful effects— the government will *have* to listen to students. If students take a stand they can achieve anything, Luvsana says confidently. For her, however, as for many other participants in the Koodankulam movement, victory translates to nothing short of the plant's closure.

Her mother, the ever-smiling, ever-cheerful, reed-thin Tamilarasi, who has joined us whilst feeding her youngest daughter, pitches in animatedly: "When they say the plant is working it's a lie. They think we are fools. There is no proof that the plant is working. Previously we saw workers going in so we knew some work was on. But now we hardly see anyone and we hear no sounds," she reasons.

What about the morale and mood of the protestors?

"We still go for the protests everyday. We won't back down. We will fight till they close down the plant, and we are confident of victory. The government is making a fool of us; it is time to take them for a ride. We will see who the fools are—the people or the government—in the forthcoming elections," she says breaking into laughter. She will support Uday Kumar irrespective of the political party he joins because "he cares about the people and is not interested in money or political power".

(This is the first of many similar responses I hear in the ensuing days from people in different villages—total, unquestioning, almost blind faith in Uday, across all political affiliations. I ask him later how he responds to such sentiments. "To tell you the truth, I have been a little depressed for the last few days because of expectations and pressure building up. I don't doubt that I will preserve my integrity but I doubt whether I can fulfill their aspirations. All I have been telling the villagers is that I will remain truthful to the people and consult them before each step. That is one thing that we have managed to do— share everything with the people, like sharing with your wife or husband. So people trust you and you don't have to carry the burden; it puts the responsibility on everyone," says Uday.)

Is Tamilarasi, loyal supporter of the movement who walks

3 km every day to participate in the women's relay strike in Idinthakarai, getting tired now, after 876 days? Are the women sitting in the Samara *pandal* dispirited after the plant went critical? How do they view the future?

She thinks for a moment and outlines their situation: "Our livelihood is under threat, so yes it *has* become tough to survive. The fishing during this period is very difficult so our men are not able to come home to eat their meals. We cook in the morning, go to the seashore with the food and also help them sort the fish. But the people's protest has not lost steam and we will never stop protesting."

The government is planning to commission Unit 2 of the Koodankulam plant. Will your protests make a difference?

She grins and replies: "When the first plant itself is not working, how will they commission the second plant?"

~

"Madam, I am Mr Sundar's PA this side. Sir has gone for field operations. I will give him your message," says the courteous voice after just one ring the next day in what has become a daily morning ritual in my quest to obtain a formal, on-site interview with the NPCIL authorities in Koodankulam. Undeterred by the continuing rebuffs, I set out cheerfully with Amal Raj, using the unreliable bus again, for the adjoining village of Vijaypathi East comprising approximately 150 houses. Vijaypathi panchayat is not to be confused with this village; the panchayat comprises 2,651 houses with a population of 10,854 according to the 2011 census. Vijaypathi village has a predominantly Thevar caste population, Koodankulam the Nadar majority caste that Uday Kumar also belongs to, while Idinthakarai is non-Nadar, belonging to the Paravar minority caste; but the struggle against KKNPP cuts across caste and religion.

At first the village appears almost completely deserted. We walk past street after narrow street lined with small houses on either side, some with thatched roofs, others that are concrete and unpainted. A noisy motorbike breaks the mid-morning silence; a few curious onlookers gather at the lone shop selling small groceries asking Amal Raj why I am talking to the owner, 46-year-old Assaq. More out of convenience than a way to escape scrutiny—though paranoia and fear of being harassed by the authorities, without cause, is not unknown in these parts—Assaq shuts his little shop temporarily and leads the way to his equally compact home nearby.

A large bed and a flat-screen Sony TV occupy pride of place in the best room in Assaq's house where his wife quickly offers hot tea and biscuits. Assaq is honest enough to admit that those who have a business—shopkeepers like him—are afraid to attend the protests because the government can "come and create a problem" and the "police can trouble us". So, even though he does not venture too far from his shop, it is an information hub where all sorts of people exchange views and sometimes, he admits, even rumours. "I am not sure the plant is working. Some people say lorries filled with diesel enter the plant... Newspapers say it is producing 'current'. How can such a big plant work without making any sounds," he asks.

Assaq feels however that the authorities will "try to make the plant work even if they have to spend more money to do so". "When millions of dollars are spent on a rocket and it fails, they correct the mistake and then send it off into space again. So people say they may do the same for the plant," he reasons. "The outside world doesn't understand. When we go for business to Valliyur or Nagercoil, people ask us whether we are still protesting and try to convince us that electricity is needed in Tamil Nadu," he continues. "But they don't realise that the plant is harmful. People who are uneducated don't realise its impact and those who are educated don't want to talk about it, they just carry on with their work."

Would people accept the nuclear plant if they were provided safeguards that they trusted, in addition to proper compensation, a fool-proof evacuation plan and other safety measures? His rebuttal is instant: "That means there is danger. Astrologers often say, 'Next year if you face a problem you will have the capacity to manage it', which actually means you will face a problem for sure. In the same way they are anticipating danger in spite of the safety guidelines, aren't they?"

So what is an acceptable option for those agitating against the plant; what should they do in the long-term; who will help all of you, I ask.

We cannot live with diseases, he says firmly. What is the use of money if we are ridden with disease? "The government says it is safe, but how can we be sure? In many developed countries, despite safety guidelines there are blasts due to leaks or other problems. As for prolonged protests this is not something which is easy, which will get over quickly, it will bear fruit only after continued effort. The government is employing many tactics to divide people, so when we have so many odds against us only god can help us," answers Assaq.

The unassailable and therefore comforting belief that god is on their side and will solve all their problems is shared by every villager without exception—it matters little if this is a last, despairing option or the first one born of faith. Another equally common feature is the all-or-nothing stance of the protestors—only closure of the plant will do. The mistrust is so great that the space for dialogue now seems non-existent; in any case, no efforts to engage in a dialogue have been made so far. Sometimes such isolation can lead to accelerated fears and misapprehensions.

"They have not started the plant yet but even then radiation is affecting women and they are giving birth to deformed babies because the thing causing radiation is already inside the plant," says 61-year-old Madelin. "She means uranium fuel loaded in the plant," explains Amal Raj.

Seventy-three-year-old Divyanandam from Koothankuli paints a dire picture of their future: "If the water from the plant is let out into the sea then we cannot fish, and secondly people within 30 km of the plant will be affected by cancer, have deformed babies and other problems. We cannot even farm. We cannot sustain our lives here, nor can we move away." As an example of the government's lax safety measures he describes how he saw a lorry carrying uranium being transported by road. "There were three jeeps in the front and back and police on motorbikes. The police asked us to move aside. It was like a tank." Amal Raj corroborates this saying that people realised much later that it was uranium that was being transported. At the time they only knew it must be something special to warrant such police cover.

Uday recalls a similar experience: "I also saw the transportation of uranium rods one evening by chance, much before our struggle began. It was being brought by road through Nagercoil from Thiruvananthapuram airport. The uranium rods were on open trucks tied to the vehicle by big chains, accompanied

by a JCB vehicle and two police jeeps. They were all going so fast
that no one had any idea what it was. No warning had been issued
in the media or through the civic bodies. People were completely
unaware. I have seen such convoys in France and they move
slowly with advance notice to the concerned communities. I do
not know the transportation code of DAE or NPCIL. I'm not even
sure they have one." The spent fuel from the Koodankulam plant
will be transported through rail and road transport "in a safe
manner without any public hazard", but such sightings instill
more fear.

Later that afternoon, walking through Vijaypathi's quiet,
tree-lined, narrow lanes with modest homes I try to find women
willing to talk to me—a surprisingly difficult task. Unlike in
Idinthakarai, the women here are not very forthcoming and
justifiably, perhaps, wary of outsiders. At the end of a dusty street,
a *kuchcha* hut has a windmill just beyond its backyard, whirring
in the breeze; a group of black goats sit under a shady tree in a
sleepy silence that seems pervasive. The women who have finally
agreed to be interviewed carry plastic chairs outside the hut for
us to sit on even as the predictable cluster of onlookers assemble
to prompt and encourage, everyone speaking at the same time!

Mohamada Bibi, 41 years of age, is reticent saying only that
the Koodankulam plant is dangerous and that she attends the
protests because she doesn't want the plant in this area. Fatima
Bibi, 39, echoes sentiments I have recorded several times in the
last six months—the plant will affect livelihoods, radiation will
cause disease, children's futures will be at risk. Her personal story
is different only in form not content. "Earlier we participated in
all the protests. I even attended protest meetings in Chennai. In
January 2013, several policemen came to our home at midnight

and threatened us, asking me to go to the police station with them. My husband was at work. How could I leave my children and go with them? They ill-treated me, harassed me till 3-4 am; my daughter who is in Class 10 still fears the police may return. After that incident I have not gone for any further protests," she says.

She too does not believe that the plant actually works, hopes the protests continue, and will "definitely vote for Uday Kumar" if he joins politics because she trusts him implicitly as "they are fighting for the people".

For many women—like Fatima Bibi—being branded by the police for merely attending a protest meeting or participating in one is a matter of personal shame, making them retreat rather than fight. Those in the vanguard of the movement however, especially in Idinthakarai, recognise this as a tactic aimed at suppressing dissent, and refuse to be intimidated.

Koodankulam's most famous leader of *morchas* (agitations), 44-year-old Ganeshan, spent 185 days in Palyankottai jail, named in 350 cases and with 108 personal cases filed against him. He claims to have been given an option to go free if he agreed to sign a document promising never to attend a protest meeting again: "But I was clear. I would fight till I die. In jail I read about Bhagat Singh, Mandela, Che Guevara," he says with pride. Today he lives in Koodankulam under the careful watch of the police. He adds that even now people cannot talk freely about the plant due to frequent police patrolling. "Nobody believes the plant is working except for NPCIL. People say the turbine doesn't rotate, so how can it produce electricity? Just a few days ago I read in the newspaper that France is planning to shift from nuclear power to solar power in the future. And here we are commencing it," he says with sarcasm.

Divyanandam declares that government response to people's grievances hasn't changed in all the years he and his fellow protestors took their concerns to the collector's office *before* the plant was built. "The government ignored us and went ahead, saying there are only a few houses in Koodankulam so the plant can be built there. They did not expect us to agitate but we did—in Kanyakumari, Thoothukudi (Tuticorin) and Chennai— and we were ignored each time. Nevertheless we will continue our protest as long as we are alive. They say the plant is working but I don't believe it. And we have god's blessings so it surely will not work," he adds confidently. There are other ways to produce electricity, the former bus conductor informs me, such as wind, solar, tidal waves, whereas if some accident occurs at the nuclear plant its effects will spill all the way to Madurai.

≈

The fishing village of Perumenal is perfect for a seaside holiday resort. The sandy beach is clean, the view magnificent, and the sea throws up more than just resplendent waves—I catch glimpses of dolphins bobbing up now and again. It's quite common to see dolphins here, Johnson informs me, watching my amazement indulgently. A short while later, regretfully leaving the idyllic panorama behind, I follow 51-year-old Johnson to the stately church, its tall spires coloured pink and green, where we settle down on the marble steps to talk about things that are not quite so idyllic. At this time of the morning the church doors are closed, its boundary wall almost touching the edge of the seashore, the unfettered wind causing the windmills in the distance to rotate gently.

Perumenal's 2,000-odd inhabitants are almost entirely Christian. Today Johnson acts as their spokesperson. He has worked for 10 years in the electrical department of KKNPP and in construction as a labourer and outlines why he thinks the plant is not functioning. "I don't believe it will work properly even in the next 10 years because it is made with low-quality material. I saw this even when I was working on construction of the bridge connecting the two reactors. For 50 bags of mud they would add only one bag of cement. When I questioned the engineer he fired me. Another time, Larsen and Toubro had built the water purification plant which was approved by the local authorities, but when an American company came to check the pipes they suggested that they be immediately replaced," he recalls from his stint at the plant. These are of course unsubstantiated allegations but there is no way to have them countered given NPCIL's refusal to grant an interview.

The engineers currently working at the plant buy their fish in Perumenal, 5 km from KKNPP; they are the primary source of information about the latest developments, Johnson discloses. "They tell us some valves are not working and it may take three years to fix the problem. They tell us 'electricity is not being produced so continue to agitate against the plant but don't tell anyone we said this'. The engineers say that if the agitation stops then either they will have to prove that the plant produces electricity or give a valid reason for its failure, whereas if the protests continue they can blame it on the protests. Engineers were not allowed to go for Sunday service in church because the authorities were scared both we *and* they would say something about the plant," explains Johnson.

Has anyone working at the plant ever shared fears about

their own safety? "A person working in the fire department told me he has shifted his family to Chennai and will follow suit because it is not safe here. I cannot divulge his name," he replies.

How do you see the future of the protest if the government continues to ignore them? "We cannot trust the government because they don't support the common man," he replies. "In spite of a non-violent protest in Idinthakarai, the police opened fire on the people on September 10, 2012, so we will be successful only if we fight, and we will fight as long as we live. Political support would benefit our movement. But above all we believe in god's help," insists Johnson.

Do governments listen to god? What can ordinary people do on their own, I ask him quietly. God has all the power, he replies.

Grandmother Madelin, 61 and ailing now, used to sell fish in the villages; she has taken part in the protests from the very beginning, travelling to Chennai and Coimbatore to spread awareness about the dangers of radiation from the plant. Living close to the plant she too discounts the fact that it is functioning and producing electricity on the same grounds of not hearing any sounds and no dischargeof hot water. "They may be repairing the plant but Mother Mary won't allow it." Madelin wants a Perumenal in which her grandchildren can live, study and become successful, not flee from the dangers of a nuclear power plant. "Our time is over, so we fight for the future," she says with passion.

The much younger housewife, 43-year-old Vincilla, parrots the single sentence: "We believe the plant will be shut down. Some say it will be closed and others say it won't, but everything is in god's hands."

The similarity in language used by most villagers in these

parts and their universal belief in god as savior and PMANE as their sole well-wisher sometimes makes their responses appear rehearsed, even indoctrinated. It is only when you spend more time with them that you realise their faith in their religion is inherent and their reliance on PMANE's leadership total. No one else has earned their respect the way Uday, Ryan, Muhilan, Father 'Mahipa' and others have; living amongst them, strategising and searching for solutions, turning the spotlight on their lives. Though the women of Idinthakarai are quick to assert that they can and will continue their struggle even if PMANE leaders were to leave in the future—a claim Uday backs vigorously albeit with caveats related to filing of RTI applications and other online work that would be difficult for the largely unlettered women to do—the PMANE influence is undeniable.

Has participation in the anti-nuclear movement also empowered these women to take part in local self-government, to take the lead in other local institutions, I ask Uday. Not much, he admits regretfully. "I would say this is a failure of our movement to some extent due to less reach, less participation. However they all exercise their voting rights vigorously and even though most of them are uneducated the literacy rate in these villages is higher than the rest of India."

≈

"This is our land, these are our people...The government makes us dance to its rules..." the stentorian tones of the local political leader do not need amplification as he gives a rousing speech, waggling his fingers at the crowd in front of him, the women seated on the floor, the men on plastic chairs in a semi-circle in the foyer of the Lourdes church in Idinthakarai. An informal meeting is in full swing and continues for well over an hour (the frequency and participatory nature of meetings conducted by the movement could serve as a model for the corporate world!). Since it is in Tamil I spend my time observing the mood, body language and demeanour of the audience, most of whom I recognise. The redoubtable Xavier Amma with her ready smile and booming voice isn't here; neither is Mary. Uday addresses the gathering at the end, thanks the speakers—he is simultaneously adept and a little uncomfortable playing the part of leader—and herds them away from the makeshift stage.

I go looking for Xavier Amma. Her daughter Pravina opens the door to their quaint home decorated with all sorts of odds and ends; she is studying for her BCom, lives in a hostel in Nagercoil far away from her mother's world, but is very proud of her. I ask if she wants to help spread awareness in her college about her mother's fight against the nuclear plant, and how she thinks she can carry the message to the next generation. She thinks long and hard and replies rather feebly that she will inform her college friends about the "damage" that can be caused by the reactor. Before Xavier who has just entered the house can step in, an irritated Amal Raj admonishes the girl: "You say you are proud of your mother and have learnt a lot from her about the protests, then why are you blankly staring at us? What is the use of your BCom? She has not come to test your intelligence but to find out whether you really understand the reason behind your mother's dedication rather than accepting it without thinking." Xavier rescues her daughter, prompting her to say: "My mother is fighting so that people can live peacefully." Then Pravina escapes into the kitchen to make tea.

As Xavier makes neat bundles of the *beedis* she has brought in just now, I look around curiously—the small alcove beyond the living room, rather, the only room, has a wall covered with lovingly framed old black-and-white photographs of family members. It is an interesting detail about an interesting woman, denoting respect for old-world values. Xavier smiles at me and I ask her gently: "You seem tired. And you weren't at today's meeting either. Is there some problem?" She replies with some of her old vigour: "Some people have problems at home but the regular people still attend and will continue to do so till the plant is shut down. I may get disheartened by family matters but not by the protests. Our protests will bear fruit. Some people asked us, 'Why are you protesting after the plant has been built'. But we have been fighting for a long time. I was 24 when I began, now I am touching 50. We are not tired. We believe in god. They claim electricity is being produced but that's not true. They are lying that the plant has opened; it cannot open...We are trying to tell as many people as possible."

Would people be satisfied if all the mandated safeguards were installed at the plant? "Absolutely not! We know it is dangerous so we will not accept it. Even the Supreme Court has questioned them so many times as to where the waste is to be disposed; their scientists have no answers," says Xavier firmly.

God is testing us, she admits wryly. If he feels it is right, he will shut the plant. However much we struggle, only if god helps us can the plant be stopped. We are ready to fight on for the next five years. For us the victory of the movement is that so many people know about it, and the plant not functioning is itself a big victory isn't it," Xavier asks, accompanying me back to the *pandal*.

G Sundar Rajan explains why the villagers are convinced the plant isn't working despite NPCIL's public announcement six months ago that it is. "Post-criticality, no sound and smoke is supposed to emanate from the nuclear plant except for that emitted by the diesel plants. But there will definitely be an increase in the outflow of water from the output channel. Every day about 700 crore litres of water will be sent in and out—this change should be visible. Here this is not happening. Moreover, even if one accepts the official statement that the plant is running it has stopped many times due to various faults. This is why the villagers feel NPCIL are trying to manipulate the whole thing."

Author Sundari has just returned from a human rights event in Puducherry where she was invited; she has been interviewed by *The Indian Express* with regard to her book (in Tamil) about her experiences in jail and the "suffering" of women inmates that she witnessed. "Now even if I die the matter cannot be ignored since it is all written down," she informs me with a pleased smile. Seated among the largest group of women at the *pandal*, Sundari exudes a new confidence; she has also assumed a more prominent position in the movement's pecking order, often acting as the women's spokesperson. "We don't know where they (NPCIL) have supplied the 400 MW that they have supposedly generated. It all seems like that joke in the film where a person says he has lost his well after taking a loan for it, and not using the money for the well at all!" she laughs heartily.

Sundari displays hitherto unseen political acumen as she makes projections for the future of the movement. "People believe god has stopped the working of the plant; we will not stop our protests. If the government continues this stand (against us) for another five years, we will change our tactics. We also know how to change our ways, not just the government—elections are around the corner, and elections are like a weapon for us." Will you support Uday/PMANE joining AAP? We will support him because he will only take decisions based on our opinions, she says trustingly.

Are you hopeful about the future of your agitation?

"Of course I'm hopeful. Belief is life. I did not know anything about politics or parties or anything. Only after joining the protests have I actually experienced society as it is. Even if governments continue to fool us, we have to continue because this will affect future generations. Life itself is a struggle; only if we struggle can we achieve something," Sundari nods.

What if the PMANE leaders go away and other support declines? She grins at me and says with bravado: "We will protest even if only 10 women sit in the *pandal*."

By this time, Milret who is being filmed as part of a UK PhD scholar's documentary research project, completes her shots and joins in the discussion. "We collected the data that showed the equipment (certain valves) is of poor quality. We submitted the details but the government refuses to believe us. They have not produced 'current' though they (NPCIL) keep hiking their claims every day—400 MW one day, then 450 MW the next. We still believe the plant can be stopped; we hear that every five days they stop the plant which means they are not able to produce 'current', so even in the future they won't and we will make sure that they stop," says a defiant Milret.

KKNPP went critical in July 2013 but, according to the NPCIL website and media reports, it was connected to the grid only in October 2013, after which it was stopped several times due to technical snags. This contributes to the villagers' belief that it is not working.

How can a small group of uneducated women influence a government to shut down a plant on which they have spent crores of rupees, I ask Milret.

"Isn't the government for the people? The people have elected these leaders—Karunanidhi, Jayalalitha and Manmohan Singh. We pay tax for what is provided to us, so they shouldn't do anything against our wishes. We have faith because we have god with us. We have gone to different places to protest, and many people come here. Nobody knew about Idinthakarai earlier but now it has become world famous. It is because of god that we have faith that we can stop the plant," says Milret.

≈

The school bell rings in the distance, signalling the end of morning classes at Idinthakarai's St Joseph's Elementary School. Scores of brown-uniformed children spill out with carefree abandon as only the really young can. Some of them join their mothers at the *pandal*, others cross through on their way home. A curious few approach me as I beckon them for a bilingual chat. Pig-tailed girls with red ribbons and flowers in their hair and inquisitive young boys crowd around as we try to understand each other. What can you tell me about Koodankulam, I ask them first in English, then in Hindi. Not comprehending me at all, they repeat their well-choreographed slogan: *"Venda venda anu ulai venda!"* (We don't want nuclear power!) interspersed with a few words of broken English, a lot of amused giggles and nudgings to *cholu*, which I have by now gathered means 'talk' in Tamil. Interrupting a session that could well have continued for a while in uncomprehending humour, Mary arrives to collect her granddaughter who is part of my little group. I persuade her to speak to me instead.

How has life changed for you and for the movement after the plant went critical in July last year, I ask Mary, who looks visibly worn out. Her response is an indictment of the state's indifference to the views of people who are most affected by the projects it sets in motion.

"There's no change as such; we continue to go for the sit-in. The government is lying about electricity being produced in Units 1 and 2 so that they get support from the people outside to sanction Units 3 and 4. When important people say that the plant is working, the people outside will believe it. When we have a problem at home, only members of the house are aware of it. Similarly, people outside do not know about the problems at KKNPP. Only we know the true story of the problems with the plant, but nobody wants to hear what the poor have to say."

What about the visible dip in their energy levels? We have some problems that we have to deal with, but that doesn't mean our intentions have faltered, reiterates Mary; we haven't become tired. "We may have some health issues because the protest makes our diet irregular. But if we are sick for 10 days then on the 11th day we will be back at the protest, but we will not stop. We started this struggle, these sit-ins, these fasts with the belief that god will help us. We have seen changes occurring because of the protest. If there were no protests the plant might have started functioning long ago. So with Mother Mary's grace we believe that the plant will be shut down. We trust god more than humans," declares Mary solemnly.

As judgments go this one is as damning as it gets.

≈

As each day goes by with no response from NPCIL's R S Sundar or his PA, I call the landline number at the Koodankulam plant, ask for the contact details of their corporate communications department in Mumbai and request formal permission for an on-site visit and interview in Koodankulam, providing a record of earlier emails and calls. Visiting the plant will not be possible at all because it requires all kinds of permissions and sign-offs which take months, I am told; I then ask for an interview with site director R S Sundar once again. "Please contact him directly," is the polite answer. And it's back to the *Aha Anushakti* ringtone, with no success. In exactly two days my visit will come to an end and I will have run out of options.

Do you feel you are running out of steam, I ask Uday Kumar at breakfast the next day, possibly the only time he is not rushing off to attend to yet another meeting or phone call or email. Despite living in seclusion in the confines of a small village, Uday follows a punishing schedule; in fact an 8 am breakfast sighting is rare since he winds up work only in the early hours of the morning. He pauses for a moment and replies: "Yes and no—yes in the sense that it is the 878th day so you cannot expect the vigour and vitality of the first week. One has to be honest and admit that energies are flagging. And no, because the struggle still continues and is taking a different turn now. So while we may have difficulties in congregating large numbers, at the same time we were able to steer through so many trials and tribulations to bring it to this stage. The fact that we have survived this long, keeping the people with us, and are ready to take a political plunge shows we haven't lost steam."

There was a lot of camaraderie last year which I don't see now; the energy is missing, large groups are sitting separately, I probe. "We have been travelling for a long time, with a lot of issues around, so the ups and downs have been difficult. Some sections of villagers are not happy with the administration in the village for their own reasons so that saps the energy of the people; also nothing big is happening right now, people are a little low. When a massive campaign is going on, people get hyped up," Uday rationalises.

He foresees a revitalisation after the general elections—he has decided to contest as an AAP candidate after discussions with AAP's Yogendra Yadav and other party leaders. The party's urban-centric agenda of fighting corruption versus PMANE's rural, specifically anti-nuclear stand is not a contradiction for Uday. He sees it as an opportunity to bring the focus to grassroots community issues.

Do you see yourself as the face of AAP in the South, I ask him. He prefers to wait for local reactions (despite already receiving positive feedback) and the party's nod before committing himself. What he does commit to is extending support to all anti-nuclear groups across the country, functioning as a bridge between them and a national political party like the AAP.

Post-breakfast, the two Australian activists and producers working for a community radio show dealing with news and information on nuclear energy and peace issues, come to bid goodbye to the PMANE team. I catch up with them for a brief interview outside everyone's favourite hot-spot in Idinthakarai—the backyard of the parish priest's residence. Gem Romuld and Emma Kelford are overwhelmed by the hospitality and welcome they have received: "This is our last day here and it has been wonderful. We did not know what to expect but they have all been so welcoming. They keep asking us if we have eaten and had three meals a day! In spite of people flooding in all the time, they answer our questions, they are interested in the struggles that we have been part of," says Gem, rummaging through her backpack to show me scores of photographs the duo has taken with Idinthakarai villagers.

What are the similarities with Australian protests on these issues, and what level of attention do they merit there, I ask curiously. "The similarity is that the poor and marginalised who are most affected by the projects are told the least and they have the least political power to stop them. Free, informed prior consent is always lacking in Australia. Australia has the most concentrated media in the world, so it is very hard to penetrate mainstream television and newspaper houses; Australia also has a corporate-owned media. Only if things are very sensational will they get on it," says Gem drily.

Whether it is a fleeting visit that leaves an impact on 'outsiders' or a lasting one that keeps them coming back for more and engaging with the Idinthakarai villagers and their cause on a regular, sustained basis till the end—whenever, whatever that may be—there is something about this movement that tugs at people's emotions. Perhaps there is an element of almost envious admiration—these women have the courage and stamina to pursue a fight that most people would not even begin, let alone sustain without losing hope; opposing the might of the state with little guarantee of success is a courageous decision.

The UK-based filmmaker who visits Idinthakarai frequently corroborates my theory: "My parents live in Thiruvananthapuram, 90 km away from the Koodankulam plant. On a basic level, I too am worried about the safety of the plant, the possibility of cancer, how it will affect my parents. But only the people of Idinthakarai are taking any concrete steps to resist the plant.

I find the courage of the women very inspiring—how can they take on such a repressive state machinery without caring about the repercussions? They may not have gone to fancy colleges but they are very well-informed and I feel I have a lot to learn from them. I feel quite powerless when I look at the immense amount of injustice in the world. But they do what they can even though they know it might take a few generations to carry the struggle forward. Struggle and protest is part of their life. Also, the love and warmth with which they open up to a stranger like me gives me more hope about humanity. Everyone is always bothered about whether I have eaten properly," smiles the young scholar.

There is an easy camaraderie between the two of us, sharing adjacent rooms in the church hospital, often travelling together to nearby villages, comparing notes at the end of the day during the daily post-dinner walk under the clear night sky. In different ways, we are both taking the story of Idinthakarai beyond its physical, geographical boundaries, into a larger world.

Young Delhi-based activist Bhargavi tells stories of Koodankulam wherever she goes—about the time Jeswin's father was arrested under the Goondas Act, or about Rajalingam or Pushparyan. "We have groups like Students for Koodankulam, Journalists and Women Writers and Artists/Musicians for Koodankulam—these were formed when the protests against the plant were at their peak (September 2012), when the police surrounded Idinthakarai. The idea was to bring people together," she says forcefully. "I coordinated the new year celebrations in Idinthakarai, the visit of the Bhopal gas victims—they could easily relate to the women here, they didn't need any translation to connect with their pain. I also brought over people from the Omkareshwar project in Madhya Pradesh whose *jal satyagraha* proved very inspirational," says Bhargavi.

Bhargavi traded in a highly-paying corporate job to volunteer and campaign for the Delhi forum, later attending CNDP meetings and finally visiting Koodankulam/Idinthakarai in June 2012. She kept coming back to "build the trust of the people", to show them that it wasn't just work that compelled her to keep visiting them but because "this is where she belonged". Meera Uday Kumar and Xavier Amma are her role models for vastly different reasons. "If I were in Meera's position, being a radical, progressive feminist, I couldn't have said: 'You go to the village and fight, I will take care of the children'. I admire her immensely. I met Xavier Amma for the first time when she visited Delhi for a workshop. As a campaigner I don't earn much so we didn't have enough money to take 10 participants in a taxi and I felt very bad making her walk. But she said: 'This is nothing, we are all working to represent our issue.' I have never seen a person like that in my life. I learnt resistance from these women," declares Bhargavi with visible emotion.

How do people respond to stories about the women of Idinthakarai and their struggle? "Some people are inspired, some people take time, and sometimes the response is immediate. When I told these stories to people in Australia they were really moved and wanted to do something."

Closer home she is still considered a rebel by her family She accepts that, saying: "It is tough for them to change and acknowledge things, but my younger sister understands me now. I have never regretted giving up my corporate job to be able to do this!"

∼

How does one check how much power the plant is producing?

My question is a valid one but it prompts spontaneous laughter among the crowd sitting in the Samara *pandal* late in the evening. NPCIL site director R S Sundar had announced in December 2013 in an interview to *The Hindu* that KKNPP was producing 400 MW, which would be further increased to 750 MW in a month. I wanted to know how one could independently verify this. Apparently this was an exercise attempted by everybody sitting around me including the PMANE leaders—with zero success.

Later, Uday explains: "There is an organisation called the Southern Load Dispatch Centre (SLDC) in Bangalore where you can check, and I sent them an RTI query but there are a lot of discrepancies in their reply. In one place they mention Koodankulam has produced x MW but they have not included it in the category of nuclear power plants (NPP); when they tally the total, Koodankulam is not included." And, according to Uday, Chief Minister J Jayalalitha has not yet mentioned power being supplied by Koodankulam.

Among the PAP nobody believes that the plant is working, I say. He nods and elaborates: "We do get an inkling that not everything is right with the plant. The prime minister has not even dedicated the plant to the country. If this man sees himself as the nuclear redeemer of India then why is he not coming here to dedicate the project to the country? It has not been linked to the grid either (according to NPCIL and media reports however, KKNPP was linked to the state electricity grid on October 22, 2013). Today I received a reply to an RTI query to the Tamil Nadu Government Generation and Distribution Corporation (TANGEDCO); I had asked them how much electricity is being produced and distributed by KKNPP but they forwarded the letter to some other agency instead of answering the question."

The absence of communication and transparency by the nuclear establishment in general and NPCIL in particular is not unusual. "They (KKNPP officials) rarely meet the press; if they do, it is most often an interaction initiated by them related to specific news they want to share with us," NDTV's Chennai correspondent Sam Daniels tells me frankly.

"The DAE has never had the culture of sharing anything with anybody. They are not held accountable anywhere, not even in parliament. It is the PMO's pet child, well-protected and well-funded," says Uday.

NPCIL, which is part of the DAE, is responsible for the operation of all nuclear plants in the country. The Indian Atomic Energy Act of 1962 empowers the DAE to restrict all information related to the location, quality, quantity, transaction, theory, design, construction and operation of reactors as well as research and technological work on materials and processes. The Supreme Court upheld Section 18 of the Act declaring that information on nuclear installations cannot be made public "in the national interest".

Interestingly, however, the NDMA guidelines (in concurrence with AERB and DAE), **mentioned in the Supreme Court May 2013 judgement (G Sundar Rajan V/s Union of India)** highlight an important concern related to the public's need to know:

> *The fact that one cannot see, feel or smell the presence of radiation, coupled with a general lack of credible and authentic information to the public at large about radiation and radiation emergencies and wide publicity given to any nuclear/radiation-related incident, has resulted in several erroneous perceptions about nuclear radiation/technology—not surprisingly most*

people perceive that any small nuclear/radiation incident will lead to a situation like the Hiroshima/Nagasaki or the Chernobyl accident.

Economics Nobel laureate Amartya Sen, in his book *An Uncertain Glory*, co-authored with Jean Dréze, highlights the lack of transparency of the nuclear establishment. Sen and Dréze state clearly that "reliable facts" about the various nuclear establishment institutions "are hard to ascertain".

The sole regulatory body of all nuclear plants in the country, AERB, has for long been criticised for its lack of independence— it reports to the Atomic Energy Commission (AEC) whose chairman is the secretary of the DAE. In effect, the regulatory body (AERB) reports to the very institution whose operations it is supposed to regulate and monitor in the public interest! Former AERB chairman and nuclear scientist Dr A Gopalakrishnan has been campaigning for its autonomy since the mid-1990s; Dr EAS Sharma, former union power secretary, also writes that unless a truly independent regulator is in place, India may not be ready to set up and operate nuclear plants safe enough for the people.

In August 2012, the Comptroller and Auditor General (CAG) tabled a report in parliament recommending that the nuclear regulator AERB become independent and empowered through a law. The CAG also slammed AERB on multiple counts--for not preparing a nuclear and radiation safety policy for the country despite clear instructions given in1983; for not developing 27 out of 168 safety documentsfor operating nuclear power plants; for having no decommissioning plan in place 13 years after issuing a safety manual on it; for having no proper mechanisms in place for the disposal of radioactive waste; for inadequate off-site emergency preparedness; for being "slow" in adopting international benchmarks and good practices. It was a long list of indictments by a government institution mandated to ensure accountability. The Public Accounts Committee (PAC) accepted the CAG report. The proposed bill for an autonomous Nuclear Safety Regulatory Authority (NSRA) to replace AERB is yet to be passed.

A day before I leave Tamil Nadu I call KKNPP site director R S Sundar one last time. He finally answers the phone and informs me firmly that an interview would not be possible at this point since "it is a sensitive matter" and that I should visit Koodankulam a few months later when it "might be possible".

On the drive back to the airport—a longer route this time via Madurai—I can't help thinking that if a Mumbai-based journalist, filmmaker and writer cannot get an hour's access to the Koodankulam plant's site director after numerous phone calls and emails providing all the requisite professional credentials, how much more difficult might it be for a villager, albeit one who lives 2 km from the plant?

I halt in Madurai to meet television executives of a local Tamil channel for a new documentary project. While leaving, I casually ask them about the Koodankulam plant. To a man, the response is upbeat and enthusiastic: the long wait for the Koodankulam power plant is finally over. Tamil Nadu's power woes will now be overcome.

Two perspectives, just 237 km apart. Which will prevail?

Chapter Seven

JOURNEY'S END OR NEW BEGINNINGS?

"Koodankulam will protect right to life guaranteed under Article 21 of the Constitution, for achieving a larger public interest... We have to balance 'economic scientific benefits' with that of 'minor radiological detriments' on the touchstone of our national nuclear policy."

—Supreme Court judgment on Koodankulam in response to a public interest litigation (PIL), May 2013

The most poignant scene in the 2004 Hindi film, *Swades* follows a dramatic sequence in which the hero Shah Rukh Khan, playing an NRI scientist on a visit to India, sets up a small hydro-electric power plant in a village, enlisting the villagers' support to build a reservoir beneath a spring on a hill. He uses his own resources to buy the turbines. Electricity crackles down the wires and a bulb is lit in the hut of a wizened old woman who peers at the light through rheumy eyes, exclaiming: *"Bijli!"* (Electricity).

Ten years later, more than 300 million Indians in 78 million rural households have no access to electricity. Six per cent of the country's urban population and over one-third of the rural population lives in homes without bulbs that a Shah Rukh Khan can come and light up, except perhaps in their dreams.

The electricity-generation scenario in India is a curious mix of thermal, hydro, renewable and nuclear energy—about 65 percent of the electricity consumed in the country is generated by thermal power plants, 22 percent is hydroelectric (plants), 3 percent by nuclear plants and the remaining 10 percent from alternative sources such as solar, wind, biomass. Thermal energy (coal, gas and oil-based) produced with fossil fuels contributes to greenhouse gases, global warming and climate change. But it remains a frontrunner in the power-generation pyramid, with most upcoming projects being coal-based.

Renewable sources of energy include wind, solar, geo-thermal, bio-energy (comprising biofuels, biogas, tidal power); among these, wind power has an estimated potential of 45,000 MW thanks to India's 7,000-km coastline as well as increased investments from the government as well as private players. The Twelfth Plan period has set a target of 15,000 MW for wind power, while the National Solar Mission announced a $19 billion dollar plan to produce 20,000 MW of solar power by 2020 as early as 2009. PMANE and other anti-nuclear activists promote this 'green energy' option.

Nuclear energy plays a very small role in power generation with a current capacity of 5,780 MW (2014 figures as per the NPCIL website) from the sole power-generation company, NPCIL. This will probably increase with the anticipated entry of private companies such as Tata Power, GMR, Reliance Infrastructure and others. Despite its relatively small contribution to the power-generation hierarchy, nuclear power is regularly projected by successive governments, irrespective of political affiliations, as the optimal way forward in the future when energy requirements could escalate enormously. Optimism is a consistent quality with the AEC, and their predictions of output are not hampered by poor performance on the ground; as the years progress so do the numbers in the prognoses.

In the 1950s, Dr Homi Bhabha, founding chairman of the AEC, announced that 8,000 MW of nuclear power would be generated in India by 1980. In 1962, the prediction was 20-25,000 MW by 1987; in 1969, the predictions rose to 43,500 MW by 2000.

The real figures were an installed capacity of 600 MW in 1980, 950 MW in 1987 and 2,720 MW in 2000. In 2007, after five decades of substantial and regular financial support from the government, nuclear power capacity touched 3,310 MW, less than 3% of India's total power-generation capacity. The current goal is to increase the existing less than 3% power generation (according to 2014 government figures)to 25% by 2050.

The DAE aims to achieve targets of 21 GW (21,000 MW) by 2020, 70 GW by 2032 and 275 GW by 2052. Their vehicles to drive this ambition past the finish line are, of course, the 20 operational reactors in six nuclear power plants across the country—Tarapur (Maharashtra), Rawatbhata (Rajasthan), Kalpakkam (Tamil Nadu), Kaiga (Karnataka), Narora (Uttar Pradesh) and Kakrapar (Gujarat).

And now, 24 long years after the Indo-Russian deal was signed, Koodankulam in Tamil Nadu is the latest addition to the nuclear armoury.

Unmet goals in the nuclear power industry, experts declaim knowledgeably, are inevitable because setting up a nuclear plant is an arduous, water- and capital-intensive, expensive process involving state support, permissions and clearances, lengthy construction time, commissioning and decommissioning costs, safe disposal of dangerous radioactive waste and multiple human interactions/interfaces and assurances that need to be put in place. Even if all of this is meticulously done, nuclear plants worldwide face the same threats of mechanical breakdown, design faults, terrorism, natural calamities, human error, and accidents.

Globally, there have been 99 nuclear accidents—civil and military—between 1952 and 2009, according to *Nuclear News*, November 2012. The meltdown of the three nuclear reactors at the Fukushima Dai-ichi plant in Japan, in March 2011, would be the 100th nuclear accident, according to this estimate.

The Three Mile Island (TMI) nuclear accident in the US in March 1979—a combination of mechanical and human error— severely impacted the nuclear industry in the 1980s and 1990s. Several plants were shut down in response to heightened public fears even though the repercussions on people's health were not serious. Conflicting information provided to the public due to communication problems (at the plant) only fuelled their anxiety. The clean-up after the accident which took place from 1979-1993, cost 1 billion dollars according to the International Atomic Energy Agency or IAEA. The TMI accident rated Level 5 out of 7—which is the highest—in the International Nuclear and Radiological Event Scale (INES) which measures the magnitude of a nuclear disaster as prescribed by the IAEA. The Chernobyl disaster in April 1986 and more recently the Fukushima Dai-ichi one in March 2011 both rated a Level 7 on the INES, deemed a 'major accident'.

On April 26, 2006, the 20th anniversary of the Chernobyl disaster, UN Secretary General Kofi Annan declared: "Many hard lessons have been learned from Chernobyl, including the importance of providing the public with transparent, timely and credible information in the event of a catastrophe."

The Soviet authorities did not, in fact, provide timely information to residents that a nuclear accident had occurred; it was only after the radioactive alert was sounded in Sweden that they began evacuating the 'mono-town' (a town exclusively for Chernobyl nuclear power plant workers) of Pripyat after a state committee found high levels of radioactivity in the area. Residents were told the move was temporary so they left most of their possessions behind, never to return.

According to the regularly-updated site related to the Chernobyl disaster on the BBC: "The Chernobyl power plant disaster released at least 100 times more radiation than the atom bombs dropped on Nagasaki and Hiroshima; much of the fallout was deposited close to Chernobyl, in parts of Belarus, Ukraine and Russia. More than 350,000 people resettled away from these areas but about 5.5 million remain; contamination with cesium and strontium is of particular concern as it will be present in the soil for many years."

More than 25 years later, no one really knows how many people died as a result of this disaster, how many continue to suffer from various radiation-related ailments, and what the duration of the long-term consequences will be. Estimates differ from the most conservative to the highly alarming—a probable 4,000 death toll by the IAEA; an extra 9,000 cancer deaths expected by the UN-led Chernobyl Forum; the Greenpeace prediction of 93,000 extra cancer deaths with other illnesses taking the toll as high as 200,000; and an estimate of 985,000 deaths (mainly due to cancer) between 1986 and 2004 with more deaths to follow, by authors of the book, *Chernobyl: Consequences of the Catastrophe for*

People and the Environment, 2010.

Nine months after the March 2011 Fukushima disaster, in a no-holds-barred article in *The New York Times*, in December 2011, physician-activist Dr Helen Caldicott, founder-president of Physicians for Social Responsibility, wrote:

> *The world was warned of the dangers of nuclear accidents 25 years ago, when Chernobyl exploded and lofted radioactive poisons into the atmosphere. Those poisons "rained out" creating hot spots over the Northern Hemisphere. Research by scientists in Eastern Europe, collected and published by the New York Academy of Sciences, estimates that 40 percent of the European land mass is now contaminated with cesium-137 and other radioactive poisons that will concentrate in food for hundreds to thousands of years. Wide areas of Asia—from Turkey to China—the United Arab Emirates, North Africa and North America are also contaminated. Nearly 200 million people remain exposed.That research estimated that by now close to 1 million people have died of causes linked to the Chernobyl disaster. They perished from cancers, congenital deformities, immune deficiencies, infections, cardiovascular diseases, endocrine abnormalities and radiation-induced factors that increased infant mortality...*

> *...Now, Fukushima has been called the second-worst nuclear disaster after Chernobyl. Much is still uncertain about the long-term consequences. Fukushima may well be on par with or even far exceed Chernobyl in terms of the effects on public health...*

> *...When the Fukushima Dai-ichi reactors suffered meltdowns in March, literally in the backyard of an unsuspecting public, the stark reality that the risks of nuclear power far outweigh any benefits should have become clear to the world. As the old quip*

states, *"Nuclear power is one hell of a way to boil water."*

In July 2013—Fukushima had by then been classified as the worst industrial accident in the world—Dr Caldicott's presentation in Tokyo 'The Medical Implications of the Fukshima Disaster' warned:

> *The Fukushima disaster is not over and will never end. The radioactive fall-out which remains toxic for hundreds to thousands of years, covers large swathes of Japan, will never be "cleaned up" and will contaminate food, humans and animals virtually forever. This accident is enormous in its medical implications. It will induce an epidemic of cancer, as people inhale the radioactive elements, eat radioactive vegetables, rice, and meat, and drink radioactive milk and teas. As radiation from ocean contamination bio-accumulates up the food chain, including seaweed, radioactive fish will be caught thousands of miles from Japanese shores. As they are consumed, they will continue the cycle of contamination, proving that no matter where you are, all major nuclear accidents become local.*

Investigation commissions and committees (including a parliamentary committee) later reported that the Fukushima disaster was "man-made", that its direct causes were all foreseeable, that the plant was incapable of withstanding the earthquake (9.0 on the Richter scale) and tsunami that followed on that 11th day of March in 2011, causing meltdowns in three reactors on successive days. The report found that the plant operator TEPCO (Tokyo Electric Power Company), the regulators and the government body promoting the nuclear power industry, all failed to meet basic safety requirements: assessing probability of damage, preparing to contain collateral damage, and developing evacuation plans. Japan's central government as well as TEPCO were also squarely blamed for their response to the disaster—"poor communication and delays in releasing data on dangerous leaks at the facility" (similar to the Chernobyl disaster 25 years earlier) and "depicting a scene of harried officials incapable of making decisions to stem radiation leaks as the situation at the coastal plant worsened in the days and weeks following the disaster".

And yet, three years after the "man-made" calamity, *Japan Times* highlighted news of hundreds of people participating in a rally in Tokyo to protest a decision by prosecutors to drop charges over the Fukushima meltdowns—which would ensure that no one would even be indicted let alone punished. An agitated protestor at the Tokyo rally shouted: "I want TEPCO officials and central government bureaucrats to eat Fukushima-grown rice!" to audience applause.

The human cost of the Fukushima disaster will not be known for years, perhaps decades, even as various forums debate the predicted number of cancer-related deaths of those living near the plant—the figures range from 100 to 1,000 to infinite. Cancer as a result of radiation exposure can occur years later. According to data compiled by the Fukushima Prefecture and the local police, and as reported in the *Japan Times*, 1,656 deaths related to stress and other illnesses related to the quake and disaster in Fukushima Prefecture outnumber the 1,607 deaths directly related to the disaster, with 136,000 people still displaced.

Approximately 160,000 people (Fukushima officials put the figure at 159,128 in September 2012) have been evicted from exclusion zones, losing their homes and possessions, living as evacuees, not knowing if they can ever return; some were allowed limited return in 2012. Physicians for Social Responsibility writes:"Radioactive cesium has taken up residence in the exclusion zone, replacing the human inhabitants. Cesium-137 has a half-life of 30 years, and since it takes about 10 half-lives for any radionuclide to disappear, it will maintain ownership of the exclusion zone for centuries."

The Japanese Science Ministry reported in November 2011 that long-lived radioactive cesium contaminated 30,000 km of the country's land space, while "precise values for abandoned cities, towns, agricultural lands, businesses, homes and property within the 800 km of exclusion zones have not been established. Estimates of the total economic loss range from US 250-500 billion dollars" according to NewsonJapan.com and Arnie Gunderson/Helen Caldicott's reports on Fukushima's on-going damage and danger. Figures for clean-up costs also fluctuate widely, from $105 billion to $250 billion since it will take decades to complete decontamination and decommissioning of the Fukushima plant.

The Fukushima nuclear disaster shocked the rest of the world into reviewing and re-evaluating their own energy policies and an unmistakable phasing out of nuclear power began. 'Before Fukushima' and 'After Fukushima' became familiar benchmarks. 'After Fukushima' Germany closed down eight of its oldest reactors, announcing a complete end to its nuclear power programme by 2022. Switzerland followed suit, deciding not to build any new reactors and to phase out all existing reactors by 2034. In Italy, 94% of citizens voted against the government's plans to build new power plants. The United States also witnessed the early retirement of five nuclear reactors since 2012; though the country continues to be the world's largest producer of nuclear power accounting for more than 30 percent of worldwide nuclear generation of electricity. France—which gets 78% of its electricity from nuclear power and is firmly behind nuclear energy—nevertheless plans to reduce its capacity by a third by 2025 and focus instead on renewable sources, like its neighbour Spain.

After Fukushima, Japan—one of the four major nuclear players in the world—closed down all its 48 nuclear reactors. According to the *World Nuclear Industry Status Report 2014*, significantly fewer nuclear reactors are in operation today than in 2010—in large part due to the shutdown of Japan's 48 reactors. Nuclear/atomic energy constitutes 10.8% of the total electricity supplied across the world today, compared to 17.6% in 1996. Only 31 countries are operating 435 nuclear power plants and only 14 countries plan to build more nuclear reactors—four-fifths of them in Asia and Eastern Europe.

BRIC countries however remain undeterred by the disaster—Brazil plans to add five new reactors by 2030, Russia aims to supply 45% of its electricity from nuclear power by 2050, China is targeting a tripling of its nuclear capacity by 2020. And India's stated goal of increasing electricity generation from nuclear power from the current 3% to 25% by 2050 remains constant 'Before' and 'After' Fukushima.

What was India's official response to the Fukushima nuclear disaster? And what were its implications for the 20 reactors run by NPCIL across the country?

A 'Safety Evaluation of Indian Nuclear Power Plants Post-Fukushima Incident' survey was conducted by a task force set up by AERB on government orders, to suggest improvements in reactor safety (this same task force recommended 17 specific safety measures for KKNPP; despite all 17 not being implemented, uranium fuel was loaded at the plant in 2012).

The safety review assured the Indian people that "adequate provisions exist at Indian nuclear power plants to handle station blackout situations..." and that "earlier incidents such as the loss of power supplies at the Narora plant in 1993 or the flood incident at Kakrapar plant in 1994 or the tsunami at the Kalpakkam plant in 2004 were managed successfully with existing provisions".

In fact, all operations at the Kalpakkam atomic energy installations (MAPS) had to be shut down since the entire area was flooded by the 2004 tsunami. And while nuclear power plants are designed to withstand natural disasters like earthquakes—Indian power plants have, in the past, operated safely during low-intensity quakes—the provisions to withstand a tsunami do not seem to inspire confidence among the people who live near them.

The most telling comments come from residents of Tsunami Colony who ask combatively: "Many political leaders try to reassure us that there will be no natural disasters here. How can they know? Can they predict the future? We have already seen what one tsunami can do to us..."

According to NPCIL, the sole operator of all nuclear plants in the country, no accident has ever taken place since the first reactor was commissioned in Tarapur in 1969. The DAE has no obligation to provide information about accidents or incidents—fires, oil and hydrogen leaks, hot water spillages—in any of their plants; information collated is therefore limited.

Greenpeace pieced together a list of approximately 20 accidents countrywide, beginning with a heavy water leak in MAPS (Madras Atomic Power Station) in March 1991 to fire alarms and smoke at the Kaiga station, Karnataka, in 2011. According to their list, the more prominent "incidents" include a Level 3 INES accident in 1993 in NAPS (Narora Atomic Power

Station, UP) where a raging fire caused a blackout and shutdown for 17 hours; a collapse during construction of Unit 1 of the Kaiga generating station in 1994, when 130 tonnes of concrete fell from a height of nearly 30 metres injuring 14 workers; a valve failure in 2003 resulting in the exposure of six workers to high doses of radiation in the Kalpakkam atomic reprocessing plant in Tamil Nadu; radioactive material consumed by 55 employees of the Kaiga generating station in 2009 after tritiated water found its way into the drinking water cooler—due to "insider mischief" according to NPCIL which issued an "all-clear" press release within two days declaring that the "workers" had resumed their duties.

In June and July 2012, workers were exposed to radiation as a result of leaks in the Rajasthan Atomic Power Station at Rawatbhata; an IAEA 'safety review team' inspected Units 3 and 4 later in the year, identifying certain deficiencies in their operations though also noting "good practices". This was the first safety review of an Indian nuclear power plant under the IAEA's Operational Safety Review Team (OSART) programme.

Deeming the safety review and assurances provided by the government post-Fukushima sufficient to assuage the fears and anxieties of all those living near nuclear plants or proposed nuclear plants, then Prime Minister Manmohan Singh declared that plans for India's nuclear expansion programme would continue, "ensuring that nuclear energy meets the highest safety standards, on which there can be no compromise". His trusted lieutenants in the DAE went ahead and confidently asserted that the odds of accidents at nuclear plants were "one in infinity or zero" (AEC Chairman Srikumar Bannerjee quoted in *The Hindu* November 10, 2011) and that "Indian reactors are a hundred percent safe"

(Srikumar Bannerjee speaking to science journalist Pallava Bagla of NDTV on March 20, 2011). This contrasted strangely with IAEA Director General Yukiya Amano's statement reported in the Indian media (NDTV's *Walk the Talk* with Shekhar Gupta, March 23, 2013): "We cannot say there is hundred percent safety when it comes to nuclear power plants...but we can make a nuclear plant as safe as humanly possible." Amano cited prevention and mitigation as two essential measures for safety at nuclear plants, along with monitoring; while specifying that the nuclear industry had a good safety record, Amano said: "The problem is that there are some accidents that are not likely to happen but when it happens, the impact is huge."

The IAEA chief also clarified that safeguards by their organisation relating to Indian nuclear reactors pertained only to preventing nuclear material from being used for military purposes, not to ensure safety of the plants, which is the responsibility of the government.

Physicist-author M V Ramana makes a succinct comment in his book *Power of Promise: Examining Nuclear Energy in India*: "The important question that underlies discussions of nuclear accidents is not whether nuclear facilities *can* be safer but *will* they in fact, be safer? The evidence so far offers little reason to believe in the latter."

In a parallel timeline however, the Manmohan Singh government continued to import nuclear power reactors, assigning four foreign firms—Areva of France, GE and Westinghouse of the US and Atomstroyexport of Russia—a nuclear park each to build multiple reactors. No construction has begun at any of these sites despite MoUs being signed in 2009. The existing nuclear liability law in India which holds the supplier responsible in case of an accident at the nuclear plant—foreign suppliers are reluctant to commit to this, preferring to put the onus on the operator NPCIL and, by extension, the Indian taxpayer—is one major hurdle these nuclear parks have to overcome; the second is grassroots opposition to the multi-reactor projects.

Whether it is Jaitapur, Mithi Virdi, Chutka, Banswada, Kovvada, Haripur—all sites for proposed nuclear power plants— the message sent out by project-affected people is loud and clear: "Not here, not anywhere; not in any country in the world." This, incidentally, was the slogan farmers and other villagers used at a protest rally in September 2013 against the proposed 6,000 MW nuclear power plant by US-based company Westinghouse at Mithi Virdi village in Gujarat. In a memorandum to then Prime Minister Manmohan Singh, on the eve of his US visit the same month, protestors submitted affidavits refusing to sell their land at any price to the governments of Gujarat or India or NPCIL; they also condemned the dilution of the nuclear liability law that would "endanger the lives of common people of India".

The Jaitapur nuclear reactor park in Maharashtra's Ratnagiri district will be the largest in the world if NPCIL triumphs over fierce local resistance to the project. Six 1,650 MW nuclear reactors with a total capacity of 9,900 MW will take Jaitapur to the top of the global list. For the people who live here, however, the issues at stake are local and immediate—fears about their safety since the site area is "in an earthquake-prone zone", concern over radiation effects on their health, damage to the environment, waste disposal plans, lack of preparedness in case of a disaster, and a lot more they will have to deal with if they have a nuclear plant in their backyard.

In Andhra Pradesh, the government plans to go ahead with

the Rs 60,000-100,000 crore (figures vary) 6,000 MW Kovvada Nuclear Power Park in Ranasthalam block of the northern coastal district of Srikakulam, with NPCIL setting up six 1,000 MW reactors with technical assistance from US-based company General Electric-Hitachi. Approximately 8,000 people will be displaced by the 'park'which will need 1,000 hectares of land. Assurances of "state-of-the-art technology" and reactors that will be able to withstand tsunamis or earthquakes or terrorist attacks have not convinced people in the Ranasthalam mandal, a majority of whom oppose the project; local elected bodies of 35 villages passed a resolution against the plant in March 2011, fearing a Fukushima replay. "We shiver even to imagine the consequences here, especially after learning how a developed country like Japan turned helpless in tackling the nuclear disaster," a Kovvada resident declared at a protest rally (as quoted in *Indo Asian News Service*, March 16, 2011). The local population in the affected villages—backed by environmental groups and activists—vowed not to let construction of the plant even begin, declaring that they would follow the Koodankulam example of ongoing protests.

When people celebrate the postponement of a public hearing it's generally safe to assume that they are not in favour of the project. Villagers of Chutka, Tatighat, Kunda and Manegaon— predominantly Gond tribals (supported by environmental groups and activists)—have long opposed the 1,400 MW Chutka nuclear power project on the banks of the river Narmada. After two failed attempts, a public hearing did take place in February 2014 amidst reports of widespread protests by local tribals who declared that"they would rather die than let the nuclear plant be built".

If a lot of this sounds familiar it is because for the people fighting nuclear power plants near their homes, the concerns stay the same and NPCIL is their common unresponsive adversary. The outcome of their protest movements is also the same—an uncertain place in a hard-fought battle in an even harder war. Sometimes the collective voice of the people—backed by aggressive political leaders—succeeds in changing the course of an international agreement such as the 2009 Indo-Russian deal proposing six nuclear reactors for the 6,000 MW Haripur power plant in West Bengal. The Mamata Banerjee-led Trinamool Congress scuttled the nuclear plant citing high-density population in the area, and environmental damage.

Sometimes people decide to accept compensation for their land and allow a nuclear power plant to be built on it. The DAE has thus acquired 1,503 acres of land for a 2,800 MW nuclear power plant in Haryana's Fatehabad district, home to several wildlife species such as the chinkara, nilgai and barasingha. The Rs 23,502 crore plant has seen a majority of farmers (854) withdraw from the four-year protest after accepting a total compensation of Rs 419.82crore. Those who rejected compensation face a tough battle.

In the post-Fukushima world and in India, additionally, in a post-Koodankulam world—with heightened awareness, access and availability of knowledge about nuclear energy, more people *are* beginning to exert their right to make informed choices or express dissent about projects that will negatively impact their future. Protests continue, loud and clear, against nuclear power plants in Jaitapur, Mithi Virdi, Kovvada, Banswada, Chutka, and other big projects.

The response of the state to dissenting people's movements has not been encouraging in the past. Will the government continue to equate dissent with sedition, as it did in Koodankulam in 2012? Will nuclear power plants continue to be foisted upon unwilling citizens?

Dr A Gopalakrishnan, a longtime critic of the nuclear establishment in India despite being former chairman of AERB, warned in an interview on Koodankulam to *India Today* online: "The government will have to learn how to handle public anger. You can't just brush it aside. People have been protesting but their voices have not been heard so far by an arrogant nuclear establishment."

Just as the Fukushima disaster jolted the world into awareness about the dangers of nuclear power, the Koodankulam struggle which began in the same year turned the spotlight on the nuclear issue. It became the fulcrum of anti-nuclear protests in India, starting small as a daily protest by the fishing community to become a mass movement breaking caste and community barriers in a relatively short span of time. After almost 880 days of daily protest at the Samara *pandal*, the spirit and resolve of the women of Idinthakarai remain as firm as their belief that the plant is not working, and that god will see that it never does.

Post-criticality however, there has been a clear shift in perspective on the part of leaders and supporters. In January 2014, there is a more realistic emphasis on impact and reach rather than closure.

Uday explains: "The outcome of the struggle is yet to be decided but the process has been successful, which is a big victory. We have made people conscientious; we have made them aware about the technical, scientific and legal issues involved. No other plant will start without the people's opinion—this is already happening in Jaitapur and Fatehabad."

"The Koodankulam movement is an inspiration for other anti-nuclear movements so there may be more trouble ahead for the government. The movement has also taken the nuclear debate public: earlier, talking against nuclear power was considered anti-national or a security issue; it was out of RTI. These people (PMANE) have thrown some light on a completely dark area. Besides, Tamil Nadu is not an ignored region as is the Northeast, for example. In fact, if the movement were situated within accessible distance of Delhi it would have got much more media attention, especially (from the) national media," says Kannan Sundaram frankly.

The Nagercoil-based editor-publisher of *Kalachuvadu* magazine has closely tracked the people's struggle against the plant and analyses both its lacunae and successes dispassionately at his elegant, old-world home-office: "The movement has already seen a lot of success so it's not like it is a zero-sum game, successful only if the plant is shut down. They have put the focus on the nuclear plant, tried to ensure its safety. They have made people raise questions based on a scientific and analytical basis, not just on rhetoric. If the plant operates, it is going to be a safer plant and NPCIL will have to be more alert. If it cannot be operated then the plant has to be closed down and all these questions will have been raised in any case. Another aspect is the notion of the government going ahead with a project without taking into consideration the opinion of the people—that has often been challenged in India, but this is the first time it has happened in Tamil Nadu. Three years on, it is also Tamil Nadu's longest-running civil (rights) movement, the first time a non-violent struggle is happening," declares Kannan.

How many people in the state or country know and

acknowledge the movement? How broad-based is it, I ask Kannan. The local leaders are supposed to mobilise people in the state and inform them about the dangers of nuclear power, but that has not really happened, he replies. "The cross-section of support across religion and caste across the state has come from people who are enlightened public intellectuals, but not at the ground level. They have not been able to win the support of people belonging to the majority caste in this area—the Nadars. The majority of these communities are beneficiaries of the development process, developing materially; they are blind to the repercussions of 'development'. The middle class is completely blind to any criticism of development. But that is the social trend here, not really a failure of the movement. Over three years, the movement has been able to open the eyes of people who opposed it in the beginning. But they are not ready to get out on the streets and fight. It is difficult for the government to control the coastal people since they are more cut-off, they are not as integrated into society as the others who may not be able to fight the system," says Kannan.

I ask Nityanand Jayaraman of the Chennai Solidarity Group for Koodankulam Struggle why the movement could not get a groundswell of support from people away from the coast, people from the majority caste and from middle class Tamil Nadu citizenry. Does the support base continue to be confined to the coastal fishing community?

"It is true that active support waned with increasing distance from the power plant. But the Koodankulam struggle can by no means be called solely a fisherfolk struggle. The inland villages of Radhapuram taluka were active in their participation in the movement, both by coming out in large numbers and financially.

However, in terms of solidarity, the fisherfolk were able to activate their considerable and powerful network to mobilise distant fishing villages to join the Koodankulam struggle. For instance, fisherfolk from Tuticorin and Kanyakumari were very vocal and active as solidarity workers. When strikes were called by the Koodankulam movement, fisherfolk from across Tamil Nadu participated in solidarity," says Nityanand.

Environmental activist G Sundar Rajan agrees about the need to expand the reach of the movement: "We have been doing as much as possible within Tamil Nadu—telling people about the impact of Koodankulam on the environment also. All the literature we have brought out is in the vernacular language. There was a *Hindu*-CNN-IBN survey conducted in Tamil Nadu in 2013 where 46% of the people polled were with our struggle and only 23% in favour of KKNPP. That was due to the campaigning. I gave talks in at least 100 colleges, schools, clubs and associations within the state. I've even travelled to Mumbai's Tata Institute for Social Studies and to Jaitapur. We should ensure coordination between all the anti-nuclear movements across the country. Other struggles have a lot to learn from Koodankulam."

"When I go back I will tell people that they have been fighting only for a short time whereas in Koodankulam people continue to fight for their beliefs for years. Awareness is being created here which we are not able to do back home; we will also try and rope more women into our protests," says Ashish Biruli earnestly at the Idinthakarai anti-nuke convention in January 2014. The 'home' he is referring to is Jadugoda in Jharkhand's East Singhbhum district where the Uranium Corporation of India (UCIL) "used to dump radioactive waste on public roads without even covering it". That changed after the protests began and people realised the effects of radiation after watching films made on the issue (notably *Buddha Weeps for Jadugoda* by Shriprakash Jaiswal), but the mining continues in the face of continued protests says Ashish. Lack of knowledge, awareness and illiteracy has added to the hurdles the movement already faces, he admits.

Ashish is a Ho tribal who was born and lives in Jadugoda "in a radiation zone...knowing I could be the next victim". He studies the problems of his own community through the camera lens, using the medium of photography to focus on those who live in the shadows. "Whatever happens in Koodankulam will set an example for others to follow," says Ashish. "People in Jadugoda are not as aware; they don't realise the situation they are facing. Shriprakash and I can come to Idinthakarai and tell people back home about what's happening, but it would be better if they are brought here to see for themselves!"

Sundar Rajan deconstructs the movement's pivotal successes: "Across the country, people's movements have created a huge debate; earlier nobody used to talk about them at all. Even as far as our legal struggle is concerned, Prashant Bhushan appearing for our case has taken it to a different level. Moreover, our legal struggle has opened up a lot of shortcomings in the functioning of the atomic energy establishment. This is a victory of the people. Before 2011, even MPs were not treated well by the DAE because their attitude was, 'I report to the PM so why should I answer you'. But now there is a major shift and people are questioning them."

Sundar Rajan continues his objective self-assessment: "We may not be able to stop this plant or stop the second plant (Unit 2), but across the country our people's movement has created a huge debate—you can be for or against nuclear power, but the debate is everywhere. Other protest movements in Jaitapur, Kovada or Mithi Virdi can learn from our struggle. Moreover, any mishap in the Koodankulam plant will make the country's nuclear programme go for a toss. So they (NPCIL/government) are 10 times, 20 times more cautious. Even if a small incident happens, it is gone. And Uday deciding to join the AAP will broadbase the struggle as there will be more people talking about it in Delhi, Mumbai and other places. Party leaders will at least talk about it."

AAP members Admiral and Lalita Ramdas strongly advocate the political option of PMANE joining AAP as the most effective and viable alternative, given the expanded, nation-wide role the movement would like to see for itself in future, taking the nuclear energy issue centrestage.

Eighty-year-old Admiral Ramdas, who calls himself "currency" for younger people to use and get inspiration from, minces no words: "Politicians are not bothered. That is why Minister of State V Narayanasamy has said 'the plant will start' 22 times. The atomic energy people are fooling their own bosses *and* the people. We may not make much progress in stopping them but at least we can slow down the process. I have been involved in many civil society movements but they have not produced answers. Even if you can sustain the movement, the fact of the matter is governments don't care. Nobody takes heed of civil societies. You need people, money, consistency and involvement, which is fine, but to have the masses with you for such a long time becomes difficult. To get things done in our country the only answer is politics. If you get into power—politics that is—if you are in control, then you can make policy decisions."

Injecting a practical note in his assessment of the movement he has witnessed from the start, the doughty admiral says: "People want the plant to be shut down for safety, but no government that has sunk in so much money will agree to it. People cannot go on fasting endlessly while the state continues to do what it wants. Though it is difficult to walk out of it, at least we can make it safe. We can be hopeful for other plants in India. The people's struggle has to be politicised or they will feel very let down. It can be diverted into something meaningful and purposeful through AAP which seems to get positive feedback from the country," he ends.

The slender and attractive veteran anti-nuke campaigner, 73-year-old Lalita Ramdas has been associated with the Coalition of Nuclear Disarmament and Peace (CNDP) and Greenpeace for decades; these have formed the organisational base of her involvement with PMANE. She has visited Idinthakarai several times, her fluency in Tamil and easy charm ensuring visible rapport with the women who chatter away with her wherever she stops in the village. Generous in her praise of the movement, Lalita feels the time is ripe for it to move out of the confines of Idinthakarai. "It is difficult to fuel the movement, to keep it going; it has taken off in many directions—right from questioning what are human rights in a so-called democracy to legal options. It has been a remarkable example of a non-violent agitation post-Independence. I have to think hard to find a contemporary equivalent where they have sustained an oppositional role and managed to keep it non-violent," says Lalita enthusiastically.

"The Koodankulam movement was most certainly a watershed in contemporary Tamil Nadu history. I have not witnessed this kind of coming together and this kind of intensity. The anti-Hindi agitation, I'm told, was as powerful and pervasive. But even in that instance the state response was not as brutal as this one (has been). This was a watershed not merely for people's movements in Tamil Nadu but also as a showcase of the lows to which the state had (sunk to) in brutalising its own people," declares Nityanand. In the caste-riven geography of Tirunelveli district, opposition to the nuclear power plant was successful in bringing together people from castes and religions that do not generally come together. And despite attempts to divide the movement along the lines of caste and religion, it has survived and grown stronger, he adds.

Whether the plant is working or not, it is going to sit there as a huge monument to India and the world that this kind of peaceful, non-violent struggle is possible, important and lasting, declares Lalita. "But now there is a role to be played beyond Koodankulam. Before December 2013 we were looking at people (PMANE and women leaders) travelling across the country to places that face an imminent nuclear threat, but AAP has captured the imagination of a large number of people, so AAP can be the facilitator and take the movement along. The fundamental issue of fighting against nuclear power will not go away anytime soon so the question will be how the movement will lead beyond Koodankulam. Some of them have already travelled nation-wide, making a huge impact, so we can accelerate the linking up of people's groups, checking for radiation issues in other nuclear plants in the country that have been operating for years, and evolving new roles at the educational level, creating a community where every child is capable of having a conversation about nuclear energy and its dangers," says Lalita optimistically.

Even within the anti-Koodankulam movement the final word has not been spoken on the outcome of this spirited crusade against a powerful state. There are differing perspectives amongst the different partners in the struggle, but the one thing they all share is the conviction that the anti-KKNPP movement has ensured that from now on the state (and Department of Atomic Energy) will take public opinion into account before setting up and operationalising more nuclear plants in the country.

The days of ignorant acquiescence to the state's diktats in the name of 'people's development' are now over; once the genie of public awareness is out of the bottle it cannot be pushed back in. People will ask more and more questions about things that affect their lives and future, irrespective of whether they get answers or not, whether their struggles succeed or not. Irrespective of the fact that asking questions can be considered 'against the national interest' by governments that may not allow meaningful public debate. In the Koodankulam movement, various players have been labelled and typecast by the state and occasionally by the media: and so the villagers who live near the plant and are for the most part uneducated (though literate) are 'easily-led', 'emotional', 'ignorant of scientific facts'; PMANE leaders are 'foreign agents' and 'manipulators'. On the other side, the government and NPCIL are considered by the PAP to be 'adversaries', evoking mistrust, misgivings and minimum accountability. Had there been any sincere mutual efforts to engage in dialogue, perhaps the divide between the perceived 'victims' and 'villains' would not be quite so wide.

For the present there is a lot of truth in the universally held (and unstated) belief in most people's mind that 'a nuclear plant is fine so long as it is nowhere near me'. The project-affected people in Koodankulam reverse this statement and ask: 'Why don't the people who are in favour of KKNPP build their homes here and then tell us how safe they feel?'

Uday emphasises that the people are a vital part of every decision right through their struggle, "We discussed topics of democracy and globalisation with the men, women and children of the villages who were earlier always taken for granted by political parties. Things were explained to them, policies were not hidden from them, the youth felt involved, the women and children felt good. A lot of credit should be given to them because they catch on easily, even the political nuances. Whenever we met the state and central government expert teams their argument was that the people would not understand the issues and we would tell them, don't explain anything to them, just listen to them. The concept of listening to these ordinary people was alien to them."

Sundari, one of the most vocal and well-travelled women leaders in Idinthakarai, counts the movement's successes with pride: "People did not even know what nuclear power was. We informed them, we made them realise the dangers of *this* plant. We also pointed out that the materials used in this plant were of poor quality. The government refused to accept this but we proved them wrong. People are now questioning all this due to our protests."

Meera Uday Kumar analyses the victory of the movement differently: "If you live with those people for three years you will find that the women over there are very intelligent; PMANE has greatly emancipated them. It has taught people to talk about different issues; it has a lot to do with society and nation-building. I know there are going to be plenty of leaders in future, irrespective of whether the plant shuts down or not." Uday's unique contribution to the movement, according to his wife who has been witness to his role in PMANE since its inception in 2001, lies in the courage he has instilled. "It lies in showing a lot of people that if you think there is something wrong then you should say it, and if you say it through the correct means you can get the point across to the other person. Don't hide because the other party is scaring you or intimidating you; you can get through if you persevere and stand your ground. That is the main thing that PMANE and others have done. You could be a nobody and still come up and say: 'This is something I don't like,' " says Meera earnestly.

After his decision to contest the 11th Lok Sabha elections in May 2014, as the AAP candidate, Uday Kumar has officially taken the Koodankulam struggle outside Tamil Nadu and Idinthakarai, his "enforced" home since March 19, 2012. He outlines his future plans: "We have prepared the next generation of leaders and fighters so even if we disappear from the scene, there are informed and knowledgeable people to take over. We will participate in the electoral politics, get a few MPs elected and have them bring up the nuclear issue in parliament."

"The way forward is pro-appropriate technology and sustainable development, it is not anti-Indian or anti anything; it is pro-people, pro-earth and pro-poor," declares Uday decisively. "I often quote Swami Vivekananda's four-fold prescription to make yourself relevant—purity, patience, perseverance and love. We have been very pure in our words, actions and character. People in the country know we haven't been receiving any foreign funds. That allegation has been completely dismissed; nobody takes it seriously anymore. They portrayed us as anti-national, that too has been completely dismissed, we are fighting *for* the country, not against it. We have also been very patient for more than three years, without giving up our cause, which touches upon perseverance. Non-violence, perseverance, patience make us more appealing to the people. Our whole campaign has been based on love, not hate. We have spoken about overcoming caste and religion for which we use a mild dose of Tamil nationalism without excluding people from the rest of the country. People come from Kerala, Andhra Pradesh and Karnataka," he concludes.

Sundar Rajan fills in the details of the alternatives they are foregrounding. "We are focusing on bringing about sustainable development through technology. The next 10-15 years are going to be the era of alternatives, whether it is alternative energy or medicine; all of these will come together to create an alternative political platform. Five years ago, people were not disillusioned with capitalism but now they are frustrated in spite of earning well. Natural resources are getting depleted, so our work is the sustainable development agenda and taking it to the people. We are working on the economics and efficiency of it," says Sundar.

Sundar presents their cost-benefit analysis of energy efficiency. The most basic principle is 'energy saved is energy produced', he says. "The average transmission and distribution loss (T&D) is about 32%, but actually if commercial loss is brought into account then it is much more. China is operating at 4% transmission loss, the US and Canada at 7%. If our T&D losses can be brought down to 15%, that much power will be saved in our installed capacity of 250,000 MW (the specified capacity today) which works out to 37,500 MW. Tamil Nadu's total requirement is only 12,000 MW. If the same 37,500 MW had to be produced using nuclear energy we would need at least Rs 7.5 lakh crore (calculated at Rs 20 crore per MW).

"In Tamil Nadu alone, if we convert incandescent lamps to LED bulbs we can save around 500-1,000 MW. The state government distributes freebies such as TVs, mixer-grinders, so why not LED bulbs? It will cost around Rs 50 lakh-1 crore per MW to save electricity and 20 times more to produce it using nuclear energy. Setting up a nuclear plant would cost around Rs 20-25 crore per MW of production capacity; coal around Rs 7 crore per MW, solar around Rs 8 crore and wind around Rs 4 crore per MW," Sundar Rajan elaborates.

Combining energy conservation with renewable energy technologies is the green, safe energy alternative that PMANE leaders and many environmental activists now advocate, as against their earlier uni-dimensional resistance to nuclear power. Renewable energy sources such as wind, solar, small hydropower, biogas, geo-thermal and ocean-based energy have immense potential in India, they feel.

Their future projections for the contribution of renewable energies to India's total electricity generation are pegged at 35% by 2030 and 54% by 2050. Despite the new and renewable energy (NRE) sector being relatively new, its share in the country's energy mix shows a steady increase from 7.8% in 2008 to 12.3% in 2013 and 13.32% in January 2014, with an installed capacity of 31.15 GW compared to nuclear energy at 5,780 MW or 5.7 GW. Wind energy is the highest component in the renewables group—at 19.1 GW installed capacity, India is the world's fifth largest wind energy producer. A popular example often quoted to provide context to India's wind energy (19.1 GW) is Switzerland which recorded 18 GW as its total installed capacity for electricity in 2009.

Green activists point to India's vast, untapped renewable energy resources—biomass energy from agriculture and forestry residue alone could be considerable. The increasing cost competitiveness of renewable energy with conventional electricity generation, its scalability and absence of greenhouse gas emissions make renewable energy a very viable option, rather than a marginal player in India's power sector. Moreover, over time, renewable energy could meet the needs of the rural poor in remote areas of the country where there is no grid or road infrastructure, since it is a distributed and scalable resource. Most importantly, renewable energy carries no fear of health hazards. Alternative and sustainable energy initiatives thus offer safe, clean and affordable ways to meet our burgeoning electricity demands.

"On a sustained platform it will take eight to 10 years for solar efficiency, wind turbines and other renewable technologies to provide a credible alternative and get fully developed for use," says Sundar. "We will focus on bringing in alternatives. Nuclear power has been happening in our country for the past 60 years, so one Uday Kumar or Pushparyan or Sundar Rajan cannot come and stop it. We know what we have jumped into; we are motivated because once people get the correct information and we are able to give them substantial alternatives, we can bring them to our side of the table. The struggle has to go on for a generation or generations," he adds solemnly.

"We have been able to steer through so many trials and tribulations, now (the movement) is taking a political turn to gain a wider constituency. I very strongly and firmly believe that we will win because our means are pure and our hands are clean," declares Uday Kumar as he dons a new mantle to fight the same battle—professor, activist, schoolteacher, movement coordinator, politician.

For the foot soldiers on the ground, the women, children and men who carry the Koodankulam movement forward almost like a tradition—mothers bringing their daughters to protest exactly the way *their* mothers took them along in 1989—the future is what the *makal porattam* (people's struggle) is all about; it is the reason they continue to raise their voices in hope, in courage and in determination.

'We want our future generations to have a good life on this land—that is why the old and the young are fighting together. We have taken a step forward now, we won't go back.'

'Our protests will bear fruit because we are fighting for our livelihood...to protect our future generations.'

'We protest because we want to make sure our children live happy lives. If we struggle now, we can be happy in future.'

'We will sacrifice our lives but save our land for future generations.'

'Life itself is a struggle so only if we struggle can we achieve something for the future.'

—Women of Idinthakarai in their interviews with me over a span of six months from June 2013-January 2014

Epilogue

In March 2014, PMANE leaders decided to take a calculated risk and leave Idinthakarai to begin campaigning for the Lok Sabha elections since Uday Kumar, Pushparyan and Father M P 'Mahipa' Jesuraj were contesting the elections as AAP candidates from Kanyakumari, Tuticorin and Tirunelveli respectively. The 380 criminal cases filed against them in the course of the Koodankulam movement on charges of attempt to murder, sedition, waging war against the state had not been withdrawn.

On March 29, 2014 Uday Kumar came home to Nagercoil after a two-year exile in Idinthakarai, living away from his wife Meera, sons Surya and Satya, and aged parents. His mother Ponmoni's "biggest wish"—to hug her son tight on his return—came true. Surya and Satya's storyteller father was back for a while, before setting off on a hectic schedule of campaigning.

The Lok Sabha election results in May 2014 saw Uday Kumar, Pushparyan and Father M P 'Mahipa' Jesuraj lose the seats they stood for; all three also lost their deposits. The Aam Aadmi Party won only four seats in the Lok Sabha.

In October the same year, Uday Kumar resigned from the Aam Admi Party (AAP) citing lack of a clear-cut policy on nuclear power projects. While deciding to be independent in Tamil Nadu and Kerala, Uday promised to extend support to AAP in Delhi.

When the BJP was voted to power at the centre in 2014, and Narendra Modi became prime minister, he followed in his predecessor's footsteps in aggressively pursuing the nuclear energy path.

A government order (GO), dated October 9, 2014, led to the withdrawal of 213 of the 380 cases filed against PMANE leaders and others (248 were cases of 'mere agitations', 140 were private cases). About 140-160 cases remain, including some for sedition. PMANE leaders still have to appear in different courts— Tirunelveli, Valliyur—with no idea when the ordeal will end.

Pushparyan chose to leave PMANE and Idinthakarai, amicably and without rancour, following differences over the movement's involvement in electoral politics. He continues to keep in regular touch with the people of Idinthakarai and fight against KKNPP and nuclear power expansion programmes at an individual level. The loss of his father, 85-year-old Mahiban Victoria in December 2013—he was not able to attend the funeral in nearby Tuticorin, fearing police arrest—haunts him till today.

The Australian anti-nuclear activists and radio professionals produced two radio programmes in April 2014 on the Koodankulam plant for *The Radioactive Show*, broadcast on Australia's Community Radio Network.

Xavier travelled to Thrissur and Kochi for the release of a book and a documentary film on the injustices suffered by adivasis.

After returning from Idinthakarai, in January 2014, I spent 18 weeks diligently pursuing NPCIL officials for a formal, on-record interview on the Koodankulam plant. After drawing a blank with the corporate communications department in Mumbai, despite repeated calls, SMSes and emails, I decided to go right to the top and contact NPCIL's chairman and managing director through his executive assistant. A similar one-way communication followed for eight weeks. No fixed day or week or month was ever promised. None of my emails were answered or even acknowledged. In fact, the only acknowledgement ever received from the various people called, emailed and messaged over five-odd months are two terse SMSes from the head of corporate communications, Mumbai, informing me: "I am in a meeting," and "I have talked to site. At present, due to their busy schedule, it is not possible for them. Regds". These were sent in January 2014 in response to my request for an on-site interview with site director R S Sundar at the Koodankulam plant.

On May 19, 2014 I called the executive assistant again for an appointment, emphasising that the NPCIL interview was essential for the book. I was asked to check with the office in June. When I enquired if I was going to get an interview at all since the deadline for the book was fast approaching, the executive assistant said: "I cannot ask the CMD for time for an interview for you in the tone that you have just spoken to me—it is just not possible. I will see what I can do in June to arrange a meeting for you." The tone apparently has to be suitably obsequious for a bonafide interviewer to ask bonafide questions about a government project that affects the public interest. I sent a final email declining the offer of a possible June interview, saying that after a five-month wait for NPCIL officials to revert, it would not be possible to wait further. I did not get a reply to that mail either.

On May 8, 2014, the Supreme Court disposed of the special leave petition (SLP) filed by G Sundar Rajan (on behalf of PMANE) in July 2013 against the Madras High Court's inability to assess whether the Supreme Court's directives for the safe operation of KKNPP had been complied with. The Supreme Court held that: "After perusing the various affidavits filed by the Respondents, we notice that the directions given by this Court are being properly addressed by the Respondents and there is no laxity on the part of the Respondents in not carrying out various directions of this Court. For full implementation of directions, evidently, it may take some more time and we are sure that the Respondents would make earnest efforts to give effect to all the directions of this Court in letter and spirit."

On May 14, six workers (three regular and three contracted staff members) carrying out maintenance work at KKNPP were injured after an incident of "hot water spillage" when a valve they were repairing began to leak hot water on them. After first-aid treatment at the plant's township hospital they were taken to a hospital in Nagercoil, 42 km away; two severely injured workers were shifted to Apollo super-specialty hospital in Chennai, 825 km away. The KKNPP chief medical officer said they had 20-70% burns. There is no hospital near KKNPP that can treat burn injuries, nor is there any super-specialty hospital anywhere in the vicinity to treat injuries from any radiological accident.

At first the plant authorities denied any accident had happened at all; after a few hours and media interrogation, they admitted that some workers had been injured. The NPCIL site director promised to conduct an investigation while reassuring the public that there was no leakage of radioactivity due to the incident. In response, G Sundar Rajan pointed out that if a 'minor accident' could happen six months before operations commence at full scale at the site, what would happen 10 years later when the equipment had aged?

Amidst media speculation that post-criticality, in July 2013, and grid synchronisation in October 2013, KKNPP had yet to generate any electricity, NPCIL site director R S Sundar declared in December 2013 that the plant was producing 400 MW which would be increased to 750 MW in January 2014. He also clarified that the unit was being operated exclusively by Indian engineers.

In June 2014, R S Sundar stated: "Unit 1 is generating 1,000 MW (24 million units a day)", providing "infirm power"—as opposed to commercial power, yet to begin—to Tamil Nadu, Kerala, Karnataka and Puducherry. Unforeseen technical problems led to the postponement of the commercial operation date (COD).

The Southern Regional Load Despatch Centre (SRLDC), which publishes daily data on the productivity and outage of all generating stations connected to the grid, reported 21 outages of the KKNPP Unit 1 reactor during the first year of its grid connection. Fourteen of these 21 outages are trips caused by faulty equipment or poor oversight or both, and can be potentially catastrophic, according to experts. From October 2013-October 2014, the reactor was under outage for 106 days and on maintenance shutdown for 64 days. In effect, this meant the reactor functioned for 195 days in the inaugural year.

On September 10, 2014, the anti-KKNPP movement commemorated the third anniversary of the intense phase of their struggle, honouring those who "lost their lives in it" at a public meeting. The women of Idinthakarai once again sent out an impassioned appeal to institute an independent, scientific inquiry into Units 1 and 2 of KKNPP, ban the setting up of Units 3 and 4 and facilitate a national popular debate on India's nuclear policy. This was the 1,120th day of their relay protest at the Samara *pandal*.

In November 2014, Uday Kumar—accompanied by a 25-member team of activists which included 15 women from Idinthakarai—embarked on a Kanyakumari to Kashmir Rail Yatra for 10 days to campaign for a nuclear-free India, taking PMANE's message to a wider public. "We have organised agitations, strikes, rallies and public meetings. The government has foisted 380 cases against us. Despite people's opposition, KKNPP is operating. The people's voice should be heard by the government," said Uday, explaining the reason for the yatra.

Commercial operations in Unit 1 of KKNPP began on the very last day of 2014, December 31, at one minute past midnight. Tamil Nadu's rate for electricity from commercial power generation at KKNPP was Rs 4 per unit, in contrast to the Rs 2.50 per unit estimated earlier.

The women of Idinthakarai escorted by PMANE leaders including Uday Kumar and Father Jesuraj ushered in the new year the same night with a midnight Mass, followed by the entire congregation walking down to the seashore where they raised their trademark slogans of protest against the Koodankulam nuclear plant—*'Venda venda, anuulai venda!'* (We don't want nuclear power).

The parish priest, Father Jayakumar, who read the midnight Mass, assisted by three priests, ended it with the special prayer that is always recited by the presiding priest at the end of evening prayers every day, and on every festive occasion: "Hail Mary, we pray to God to protect us from the nuclear plant near our home. We ask God to shut down the plant."

As dawn breaks on the first day of January 2015, the deacon Brother Viniston writes Day 1,232 on the board in the temporary absence of Amal Raj Leon.

The leaders of the movement no longer live in Idinthakarai; Uday Kumar visits the village once a week. Mary, Sundari, Milret take turns to address the daily 4 pm briefings, to motivate the 15-20 women who faithfully sit at the Samara *pandal* today. Nothing has changed for us, they say, we are still close to the nuclear domes, our lives go on...Only the fear has increased. The *makal porat* (people's struggle) continues as the women promised it would, "even if there are only 10 of us sitting in the protest *pandal*".

Publisher's Note

In January 2015, Unit 2 of the Koodankulam plant (construction for this plant began in 2002, at the same time as Unit 1) is 97% complete, according to NPCIL. Commercial operation for this unit, slated for 2008, has been postponed till the unit reaches first criticality, now scheduled for April 2015.

India and Russia signed an agreement to go ahead with Units 3 and 4, following which NPCIL and its Russian counterpart Atomstroyexport signed a General Framework Agreement for its construction, at a cost of Rs 39,747 crore, more than twice the cost of Units 1 and 2 (Rs 17,270 crore). They are expected to be commissioned in 2020-2021.India and Russia also signed a vision document for construction of 12 Russia-built nuclear reactors in India by 2035.

US President Barack Obama's visit to India led to what he called a "breakthrough" Indo-US nuclear deal, which, simply put, lifts the onus of liability in case of a nuclear accident from the supplier—US or Russian or French companies that build reactors in India—and places it back on the operator, in this case NPCIL. The earlier Civil Liability for Nuclear Damages Act (CLND) 2010 did hold multinational nuclear suppliers accountable in case of an accident in any of their reactors. The Indian government will now establish an insurance pool with a maximum supplier liability of Rs 1,500 crore. No individual victim can sue any foreign company in case of a nuclear accident; only the operator NPCIL has the "right to recourse" to do that, and that too is not "mandatory" and is limited only to a duration of five years. The details of this "breakthrough" deal are still being worked out; international companies such as Westinghouse and others are reading the fine print before taking action.

The Narendra Modi-led government pledged that it would triple nuclear power generation in the country in the next decade.

According to the Ministry of Power's figures on total installed capacity of power on June 30, 2015, nuclear power accounted for 2.1 percent. Thermal at 69.6 percent, Hydro (Renewable) at 15.3 and Renewable Energy Sources accounted for 13.0 percent of the mix.

Fukushima update

In early August 2015, a Japanese citizens' judicial committee overruled government prosecutors and forced them to bring three former executives of the Tokyo Electric Power Co. (TEPCO) to trial on charges of criminal negligence for their inability to prevent the 2011 nuclear disaster at the Fukushima Daiichi nuclear power plant.

Later in the month, Kyushu Electric Power company re-started the Sendai nuclear power reactor amidst fierce protests in Japan.

KKNPP update continues :

A government statement issued on August 6, 2015 declared that work on units 3 and 4 of the KKNPP would start in that year as administrative approval and financial sanction had been accorded to the project.

On August 19, 2015, 100 anti-KKNPP protestors appeared in court in Valliyoor, Tamil Nadu asking for the criminal cases (filed against them for anti-nuclear agitation) to be dropped;

Uday Kumar, Muhilan, Pushpryan and Father Mahipa Jesuraj were among those who appeared at the trial court. Uday Kumar, PMANE coordinator, alleged that, "Since a portion of the spent fuel is being removed from the first reactor of KKNPP and it would be kept on the same premises, people living in the nearby villages are in a state of shock and fear. Hence it is expected that the anti-nuclear protests will become intense once again. Against this back-drop the state government-by expediting the trial of criminal cases filed against protestors-is attempting to stifle the ongoing agitation. We will approach the higher courts to quash all these cases".

On August 22, 2015, the protestors sitting in the Samara pandal chalked up Day 1472 of their peaceful, non-violent struggle.

The Tamil Nadu State government informed the Madras High Court in December 2015 that all 248 cases pending against the anti-Koodankulam Nuclear Power Plant activists had been closed. (source : Suresh Kumar, *The Hindu*, December 29, 2015)

India and Russia signed 16 significant agreements during Prime Minister Narendra Modi's December 24, 2015 Moscow visit, including nuclear cooperation. In the atomic field, the two sides signed a significant agreement for "Localisation of Manufacturing in India for Russian-Designed Nuclear Reactor Units" to enable participation of Indian firms under the 'Make-in-India' programme.

Affirming that their cooperation in the peaceful uses of nuclear energy is a cornerstone of the Russia—India strategic partnership, the two leaders appreciated the progress made in the Kudankulam Nuclear Power Project and agreed to expedite the implementation of ongoing and upcoming projects there.

In the joint press statement with President Putin, Prime

Minister Modi said, "The pace of our cooperation in nuclear energy is increasing. We are making progress on our plans for 12 Russian nuclear reactors at two sites".

Russian President Vladimir Putin said Unit 2 of the Kudankulam atomic plant in Tamil Nadu, being built by Russia, will be commissioned within weeks and negotiations are at an advanced staged for Unit III and IV. (source : *The Hindu*, December 25, 2015)

Jitendra Singh, Union Minister handling the department of Atomic Energy, declared in the Lok Sabha that Unit 1 of the Koodankulam power plant is under a shut-down 'on a regular basis for checks and other things' and will be re-started by January 2016 while Unit 2 is expected to be commissioned by March or April 2016. (source : Press Trust of India, December 14, 2015)

In her speech at the 26th Southern Zonal Council meet, Tamil Nadu Chief Minister J Jayalalitha drew the Centre's attention to the fact that the Koodankulam nuclear power plant (Unit 1) that started commercial operations on December 31, 2014 had been shut down for maintenance work since June 24, 2015.

"The Nuclear Power Corporation of India Ltd is yet to clearly indicate when the Kudankulam Nuclear Power Plant Unit-I will recommence production; we therefore request that the NPCIL may be instructed to recommence production in Koodankulam Unit-I early to meet the Tamil Nadu grid demand" she said in her speech, read out by Tamil Nadu Finance Minister O Panneerselvam. (source : *Business Standard*, December 12, 2015)

References

Background of KKNPP: 'India's Nuclear Power Problem', Monamie Bhadra in *The Cairo Review of Global Affairs*, December 2011; 'Twenty years of resistance at Koodankulam', Patibandla Srikant, Infochange.org, September 2011

Tirunelveli district information: District Inland and Marine Fisheries Department-Tirunelveli and Radhapuram; Tirunelveli district- ENVIS centre, Tamil Nadu

September 10, 2012 incident: 'Fact-finding team's visit to Idinthakarai', Kalpana Sharma, senior journalist, B G Kolse-Patil, former judge of the Bombay High Court and R N Joe D'Cruz, Tamil writer from Chennai

S A Bhardwaj, director, technical, NPCIL, quoted from 'Koodankulam Meltdown' *Down to Earth*, April 15, 2012

Impact of tsunami: Statistics culled from Government of India, Ministry of Home Affairs Report, May 25, 2005; 'Tsunami: Impact and damage - Tamil Nadu Government', Tamil Nadu government, 2005

Swapnesh Malhotra, head of public awareness division, DAE, quoted in 'Koodankulam Meltdown', *Down to Earth*, April 1-15, 2012

Agitation of March 2012: 'Fact-finding report on suppression of democratic dissent in anti-nuclear protests', April 2012. Team led by Sam Rajappa, senior journalist, Dr Gladston Xavier, senior lecturer, Porkodi Karnan, high court advocate, Madurai bench, and N Mahadevan Thambi and P Rajan, PUCL members

Jal Satyagraha: 'Protestors offer Jal Satyagraha in Koodankulam', *The Times of India*, September 14, 2012

Graveyard protests: 'Koodankulam: anti-nuke protests shift to grave-yards', Firstpost, September 25, 2012

Independent review of KKNPP post-Fukushima: 'India must put nuclear power on hold', Praful Bidwai, Rediff.com, April 9, 2011

P C Alexander statement on KKNPP: 'In the eye of the storm', K P Sunil, *The Illustrated Weekly of India*, March 12, 1989

Absence of EIA studies for Unit 1 and 2: 'Violating letter and spirit: Environmental clearances for Koodankulam reactors', Divya Badami Rao and M V Ramana, *Economic and Political Weekly*, December 20, 2008

Fukushima evacuation up to 40 km: 'Costs and consequences of the Fukushima Daiichi Disaster', Steven Starr, October 31, 2012, Environmental Health Policy Institute, Physicians for Social Responsibility;Special Leave Petition filed in Supreme Court by G Sundar Rajan, September 2012

R S Sundar interview on number of staff at the site hospital at KKNPP: 'Koodankulam produces 24 million units of power a day', A Ganesh Nadar, Rediff.com, June 26, 2014

Sergei Shutov, Zio-Podulsk's procurement director's arrest for corruption: 'Rosatom-owned company accused of selling shoddy equipment to reactors at home and abroad, pocketing profits', published in Bellona, February 28, 2012, by Bellona Foundation, an international NGO based in Norway

Nuclear liability and insurance: FAQs on CLND, 2010, Ministry of External Affairs, Government of India, February 8, 2015

Indo-Russian secret agreement of 2008 and no liability to supplier for KKNPP 1 and 2: 'India and Russia fail to resolve issue of liability', *The Hindu*, October 20, 2013; 'A request to the Russian president on his visit to India', Dianuke.org, March 27, 2012

Sekhar Basu, Director, BARC, on reprocessing of nuclear waste: 'Our policy is to reprocess all the fuel put into a nuclear reactor', R Prasad, *The Hindu*, October 28, 2012

Cost of Fukushima disaster: 'Japan's nuclear crisis: Fukushima Daiichi status report', www.greenpeace.org , February 2015

Power shortages in Tamil Nadu: 'Power-less in Tamil Nadu: No electricity for 16 hours in many parts', NDTV, Sam Daniels, October 22, 2012; 'In Tamil Nadu power cuts that last the better part of the day', September 4, 2013

CAG report on AERB, August 22, 2012: ' CAG pulls up AERB for not preparing nuclear safety policy', P Sunderarajan, *The Hindu*, August 24, 2012

Electricity and energy statistics: Electricity sector in India (Wikipedia), Government of India-Central Electrical Authority (CEA), indianpowersector.com

Facts and figures on wind energy: www.energynext.in; solar energy: indianpowersector.com

Renewable energies: 'India achieves 12.95 % of renewable energy potential', June 5, 2014, *Business Standard*, Wikipedia

Facts, figures and forecasts on nuclear power: NPCIL website (www.npcil.nic.in); India's three-stage nuclear programme on Wikipedia

https://en.wikipedia.org/wiki/India's_threestage_nuclear_power_programme?

'NPEC-Nuclear power in India: Failed past, dubious future', M V Ramana, Non-proliferation Policy Education Center (NPEC), www.npolicy.org/article.php?aid=333&rtid=2

Kofi Annan quote on Chernobyl: 'UN marks 20th anniversary of Chernobyl disaster with calls of never again', UN News Centre, April 26, 2006,www.un.org/apps/news/story. asp?NewsID=18251?

Chernobyl disaster: BBC News news.bbc.co.uk/2/shared/spl/hi/guides/456900/.../nn3page1.stm?

Chernobyl disaster (Wikipedia) https://en.wikipedia.org/wiki/Chernobyl2020

Fukushima evacuees: 'The situation at Fukushima', World Nuclear Organisation

www.world-nuclear.org/Features/Fukushima/Situation-at-Fukushima/?

'After Fukushima' decline of nuclear power plants worldwide: 'Nuclear power in a post-Fukushima world', Mycle Schneider, Antony Froggatt and Steve Thomas, in 'The world nuclear industry status report 2010-11', Worldwatch Institute

www.worldwatch.org/nuclear-power-after-fukushima?

'The world nuclear industry status report' for the years 2012 and 2013, Mycle Schneider and Antony Froggatt

https://en.wikipedia.org/wiki/World_Nuclear_Industry_Status_Report?

www.worldnuclearreport.org/World-Nuclear-Report-2013.html?

International Energy Outlook 2013 www.eia.gov/forecasts/ieo/pdf/0484(2013).pdf

MAPS (Kalpakkam) flooding in 2004: 'Work hit at Kalpakkam atomic energy site', ET Team, *Economic Times*, December 28, 2004

Rawatbhata nuclear power plant 'leaks' in Rajasthan: 'Rawatbhata nuclear power station reports another tritium leak', Sunny Sebastian, *The Hindu*, July 25, 2012

Mithi Virdi protest: 'Thousands protest in Gujarat against Mithi Virdi nuclear project as the PM heads to US', September 24, 2013, Dianuke.org; 'India state of the environment report: the monthly overview, September 2013, indiaenviron-mentportal.org (Centre for Science and Environment)

Jaitapur protest:Wikipaedia

https://en.wikipedia.org/wiki/Jaitapur_Nuclear_Power_Project?

Greenpeace.org

www.greenpeace.org/india/en/.../Jaitapur-nuclear-power-plant/?

Chutka, Banswada protest:

'Public hearing on MP's Chutka nuclear power project cancelled', ShashikantTrivedi, *Business Standard*, May 24,2013

'Over 4,000 villagers at hearing on Chutka nuclear power project: but hearing cancelled', Nuclear-news.net, May 25, 2013

Fatehabad protest and settlement: 'One man's fight against nuclear power', Sai Manish, *Tehelka*, July 2, 2013

Jadugoda: 'Jadugoda: Drowning in nuclear greed', Ashish Birulee, *Galli* magazine, June 16, 2013

Epilogue

'Hot water spillage' accident of May 14, 2014 at KKNPP: 'NPCIL dismisses reports of blast at Koodankulam plant', PTI, Chennai, *Indian Express*, May 14, 2014; 'Report on the 14 May incident at the Koodankulam nuclear power plant', VT Padmanabhan, R Ramesh, V Pugazhendi, Raminder Kaur and Joseph Makolil, June 15, 2014, countercurrents.org

www.countercurrents.org/kknp150614.pdf?

R S Sundar (site director KKNPP interview): 'Koodankulam produces 24 million units of power a day', A Ganesh Nadar, Rediff.com, June 26, 2014

KKNPP generation capacity quote by R S Sundar: 'Koodankulam produces 24 million units of power a day', A Ganesh Nadar, Rediff.com, June 26, 2014

SLRDC reports of 21 outages of KKNPP in the first year of grid connection: 'What speaks the speaking tree? Koodankulamnuclear reactor during its one year of grid connection', VT Padmanabhan, R Ramesh, V Pugazhendi, & Joseph Makkoli, November 3,2014, Countercurrents.org

www.academia.edu/.../What_speaks_the_speaking_tree_ Performance_analysis_of_kudankulam_reactor_

Commercial operations begin at KKNPP unit 1 at Rs 4 per unit: 'Commercial power generation begins at Koodankulam', special correspondent, *The Hindu*, December 31, 2014

ENG-12

Publisher's Note

Indo-US breakthrough deal: 'India and US announce nuclear breakthrough after Modi-Obama talks', HT Correspondent, *The Hindustan Times*, January 26, 2015; 'N-deal logjam cleared: Modi, Obama agree not to dilute liability law', *The Hindu*, January 26, 2015; Ministry of External Affairs, Government of India (FAQs on CLND 2010 and other issues, February 8, 2015)

Fukushima trial: 'Tepco officials are going on trial for the Fukushima meltdown', Andy Tulley, *Business Insider*, August 4, 2015

Sendai nuclear power plant re-starts in Japan: 'Japan reactor restarted amidst protests', AP, *Taipei Times*, August 13, 2015

Units 3 and 4 of KKNPP due to start in 2015: 'Work on Units 3, 4 at Koodankulam to begin this year', Zee News, August 6, 2015; 'Work on Units 3, 4 at Koodankulam to begin this year', *Economic Times*, August 6, 2015

Protestors at Valliyoor trial court: 'Anti-nuke protestors appear before court', special correspondent, *The Hindu*, August 19, 2015

General references

Dianuke.org

The Hindu

Frontline

Tehelka

Business Standard

Ndtv, Chennai

Kafila

Washington Post, Brahma Chellaney in *The Hindu*

Yahoo news ('Inside the republic of Koodankulam'Prajnya K, Grist media

Dr A Gopalakrishnan, *New Indian Express*, 'Resolve Koodankulam issues', April 19, 2013

Kractivist.org